BIG DATA ON REAL-WORLD APPLICATIONS

Edited by **Sebastian Ventura Soto, José M. Luna** and **Alberto Cano**

Big Data on Real-World Applications
http://dx.doi.org/10.5772/61396
Edited by Sebastian Ventura Soto, José M. Luna and Alberto Cano

Contributors

Mohammad Lutfi Othman, Ishak Aris, Ananthapadmanabha Thammaiah, Christos Vaitsis, Vasilis Hervatis, Nabil Zary, Sacha Satram-Hoang, Carolina Reyes, Deborah Hurst, Khang Hoang, Bruno Medeiros, Jing-Song Li, Yi-Fan Zhang, Yu Tian, Bradley Erickson

Published by InTech

Janeza Trdine 9, 51000 Rijeka, Croatia

Publishing Process Manager Dajana Pemac

Technical Editor SPi Global

Cover InTech Design team

First published July, 2016
Printed in Croatia

Additional hard copies can be obtained from orders@intechopen.com

Big Data on Real-World Applications, Edited by Sebastian Ventura Soto, José M. Luna and Alberto Cano
p. cm.
Print ISBN 978-953-51-2489-4
Online ISBN 978-953-51-2490-0

For EU product safety concerns:
IN TECH d.o.o., Prolaz Marije Krucifikse Kozulić 3, 51000 Rijeka, Croatia,
info@intechopen.com or visit our website at intechopen.com.

Meet the editors

Sebastián Ventura received his BSc and PhD degrees in science from the University of Cordoba, Spain, in 1989 and 1996, respectively. He is currently a full-time professor of Computing Science and Artificial Intelligence at the University of Cordoba, where he heads the Knowledge Discovery and Intelligent Systems Research Laboratory. He has published more than 200 papers in journals and scientific conferences, and he has edited three books and several special issues in international journals. He has also been engaged in 12 research projects (being the coordinator of four of them) supported by the Spanish and Andalusian governments and the European Union. His main research interests are in the fields of machine learning, data mining, data science, big data, soft computing, and their applications.

Dr. Jose M. Luna received his PhD in Computer Science in January 2014. He has published 17 journal articles in highly prestigious international journals and is the author of the book "Pattern Mining with Evolutionary Algorithms". Additionally, he has written two book chapters and published almost 30 articles in international and national conferences. His h-index is 11, and his papers have been cited more than 400 times according to Google Scholar.

Alberto Cano is an assistant professor in the Department of Computer Science at the Virginia Commonwealth University, USA, where he heads the High-Performance Data Mining Lab. He received his PhD degree in Computer Science from the University of Granada (Spain) in 2014 and MSc degree from the University of Cordoba (Spain) in 2010. His research is focused on machine learning, data mining, soft computing, parallel computing, and general purpose GPU systems. He has published 17 articles in international journals, 12 contributions to international conferences, and 2 book chapters, and he has served as a member of the technical program committee in more than 60 international conferences.

Contents

Preface

As technology advances, high volumes of valuable data are generated day by day in modern organizations. The management of such huge volumes of data has become a priority in these organizations, requiring new techniques for data management and data analysis in Big Data environments. These environments encompass many different fields including medicine, education data, and recommender systems.

The term Big Data is being increasingly used almost everywhere and by everyone nowadays. This buzzword is related to the emerging techniques used to manage, explore, and make sense huge volumes of data that cannot be handled by traditional techniques.

This book brings together some of the most interesting fields in which Big Data is essential. The aim of the book is to provide the reader with a variety of fields and systems where the analysis and management of massive datasets are crucial. This book describes the importance of the Big Data era and how existing information systems are required to be adapted to face up the problems derived from the management of massive datasets.

The book is divided into a series of chapters including a detailed description about the importance of Big Data in different fields. The book includes an important analysis about the significance of Big Data in hospital information systems. The complex, distributed, and highly interdisciplinary nature of medical data has underscored the limitations of traditional data analysis capabilities of data accessing, storage, processing, analyzing, distributing, and sharing. The analysis is also extended in another chapter to examine patient characteristics, treatment patterns, and survival among the elderly with acute myeloid leukemia.

The book also includes a different and interesting field in which the term Big Data is the cornerstone, the educational field. The book includes different analyses to provide insights to different stakeholders and thereby foster data-driven actions concerning quality improvement in education.

The reader will verify that, depending on the application domain, the size of data can vary from megabytes to petabytes, and the term Big Data may refer to different sizes and types depending on the context. However, regardless of the application domain, the common challenge is the same, that is, to being able to make sense of the data by processing them in a high analytical level.

Sebastian Ventura
Professor in Computer Science and Artificial Intelligence
University of Cordoba
Cordoba (SPAIN)

Chapter 1

Novel Rule Base Development from IED-Resident Big Data for Protective Relay Analysis Expert System

Mohammad Lutfi Othman, Ishak Aris and
Thammaiah Ananthapadmanabha

Additional information is available at the end of the chapter

http://dx.doi.org/10.5772/63756

Abstract

Many Expert Systems for intelligent electronic device (IED) performance analyses such as those for protective relays have been developed to ascertain operations, maximize availability, and subsequently minimize misoperation risks. However, manual handling of overwhelming volume of relay resident big data and heavy dependence on the protection experts' contrasting knowledge and inundating relay manuals have hindered the maintenance of the Expert Systems. Thus, the objective of this chapter is to study the design of an Expert System called Protective Relay Analysis System (PRAY), which is imbedded with a rule base construction module. This module is to provide the facility of intelligently maintaining the knowledge base of PRAY through the prior discovery of relay operations (association) rules from a novel integrated data mining approach of Rough-Set-Genetic-Algorithm-based rule discovery and Rule Quality Measure. The developed PRAY runs its relay analysis by, first, validating whether a protective relay under test operates correctly as expected by way of comparison between hypothesized and actual relay behavior. In the case of relay maloperations or misoperations, it diagnoses presented symptoms by identifying their causes. This study illustrates how, with the prior hybrid-data-mining-based knowledge base maintenance of an Expert System, regular and rigorous analyses of protective relay performances carried out by power utility entities can be conveniently achieved.

Keywords: association rule, data mining, digital protective relay, expert system, power system protection analysis, rough set theory

1. Introduction

According to the IEEE Working Group D10 of the Line Protection Subcommittee, Power System Relaying Committee, Expert Systems have been proposed since early 1980s to be potential tools for engineers to develop intelligent performance analysis systems for the intelligent electronic devices (IEDs) such as protective relays [1]. Some of the works where protection performance analyses can be identified are in the area of offline tasks such as settings coordination, post-fault analysis, and fault diagnosis [2–13].

Kezunovic et al. [6] explain the substation automated fault analysis using Expert System method based on the retrieved disturbance data acquired by digital fault recorders (DFRs). This fault analysis helps protection engineers identify the correctness of protective relay operation. **Figure 1** illustrates the block diagram of the Expert System. The knowledge base in the CLIPS (an Expert System shell) rules used in the forward chaining inference engine using processed data is built by interviewing experts, using an empirical approach based on Electromagnetic Transient Program (EMTP) simulation and utilizing actual big field substation data.

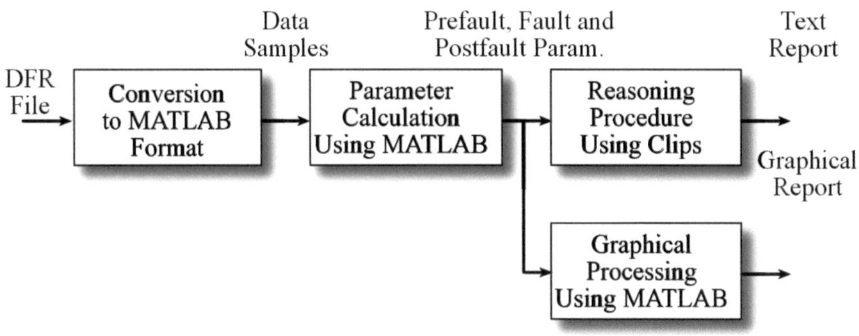

Figure 1. The Expert System block diagram [6].

Luo and Kezunovic's [10] implementation of the Expert System in automated protection analysis is more specifically tailored at detailed analysis of a specific protective relay by relying on recorded big data found only within it. **Figure 2** illustrates the block diagram of the analysis system created based on CLIPS language within Visual C++ framework. The analysis system is developed revolving around the strategy of comparing predicted (hypothesized) and actual (factual) protection operation in terms of statuses and corresponding timings of logic operands. Any matching between the predicted and actual protection operations validates the correctness of the actual status and timing of that operand. Otherwise, certain misoperation is identified, and diagnosis is initiated to trace the reasons. Predicted statuses and timings of active logic operands are basically a hypothesization of relay operations, which is done by way of forward chaining reasoning. They form the knowledge base in the rules used in the CLIPS inference engine.

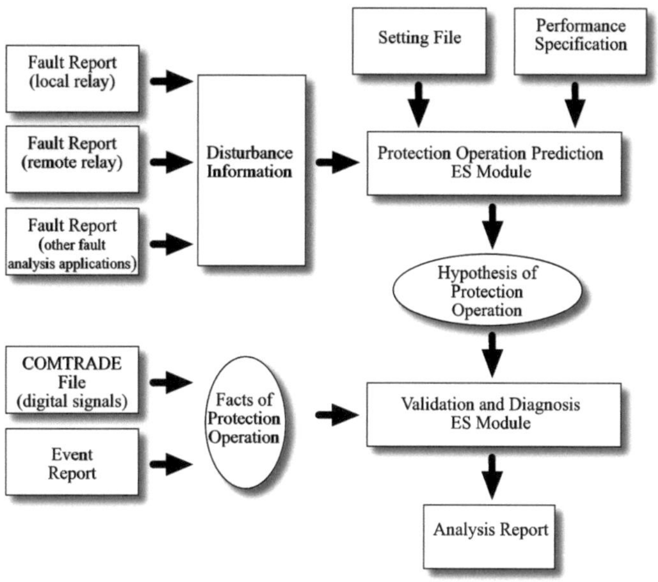

Figure 2. The Expert System block diagram for validation and diagnosis of protective relay [10].

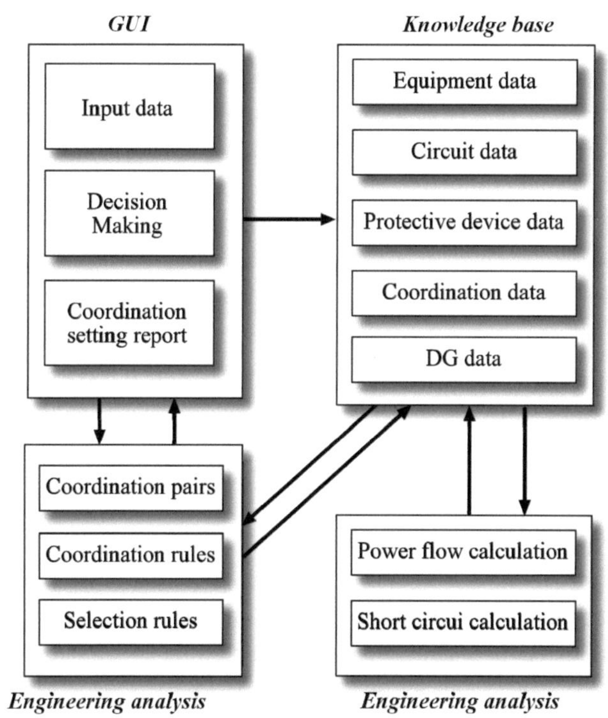

Figure 3. Structure of Expert System for protection coordination [13].

Tuitemwong and Premrudeepreechacharn [13] implement ES analysis for improving protection coordination settings of protective devices in distribution system under the presence of distributed generators (DG). By way of selecting suitable protection coordination settings, this analysis system determines the correct protection system performance in a DG-present power distribution system. The proposed structure of ES is shown in **Figure 3**. The inference engine uses coordination rules and selection rules to generate satisfactory coordination settings based on the processed equipment data, circuit data, protection data, and DG data in the knowledge base. In the case of conflicting settings, the user can make his own decision. The rules are set for the specific distribution system protection and maybe changed when necessary.

The common problem with the aforementioned implementation of rule-based Expert System in protection system analysis is the difficult upgrading of its knowledge base that is made up of "if-then" rules used for decision-making inference engine. Upgrading by expansion and refinement are necessary so as to adapt the Expert System to the continuously changing power network topologies, protection strategies, and multiplicity in protective relay functions [14]. However, acquiring knowledge of relay operation characteristics for upgrading of the knowledge base has not been an easy task due to

i. the burdensome manual handling of voluminous protective relay stored data and

ii. the heavy dependence on the protection experts' differing knowledge and inundating relay manuals.

It is beneficial if a novel technique could be formulated so as to relieve the untoward effort needed to acquire knowledge in building and maintaining the knowledge base. This technique should allow adjustment of knowledge base by training a protective relay device for as many disturbances as exhaustively possible in order to produce a complete inventory of rules. To help realize this, the authors' previous work of an integrated data mining approach under the Knowledge Discovery in Database (KDD) framework shall be the prior step before the eventual Expert System knowledge base upgrading strategy is subsequently performed [15–17].

2. Integrated data mining approach to hypothesize expected relay behavior from recorded relay event report

Under the KDD framework, Othman et al. [15–17] investigate the implementation of a novel integrated data mining approach under supervised learning in order to discover the knowledge (or "hypothesize") and the expected relay behavior. This knowledge extraction from the resident large event reports of a digital distance protective relay comes in the form of association rules as shown in **Figure 4**. The integrated data mining encompasses the adoption of the following computational intelligence methods:

i. Rough set theory: Used to *select* the minimal subsets (i.e., reduction) of attributes while maintaining the original syntax of the relay's big data of event report.

http://dx.doi.org/10.5772/63756

ii. Genetic algorithm: Used to *explore* the optimal sets of the above subsets of reduced attributes from which simple yet accurate prediction rules (i.e., decision algorithm) can be constructed.

iii. Rule quality measure: Used to *extract* the pertinent association rule from a host of the above original population of prediction rules to determine tripping logic of relay upon fault detection. This is what is referred as hypothesization of protective relay operation. This final version of knowledge representation shall be the main constituent for the Expert System knowledge base.

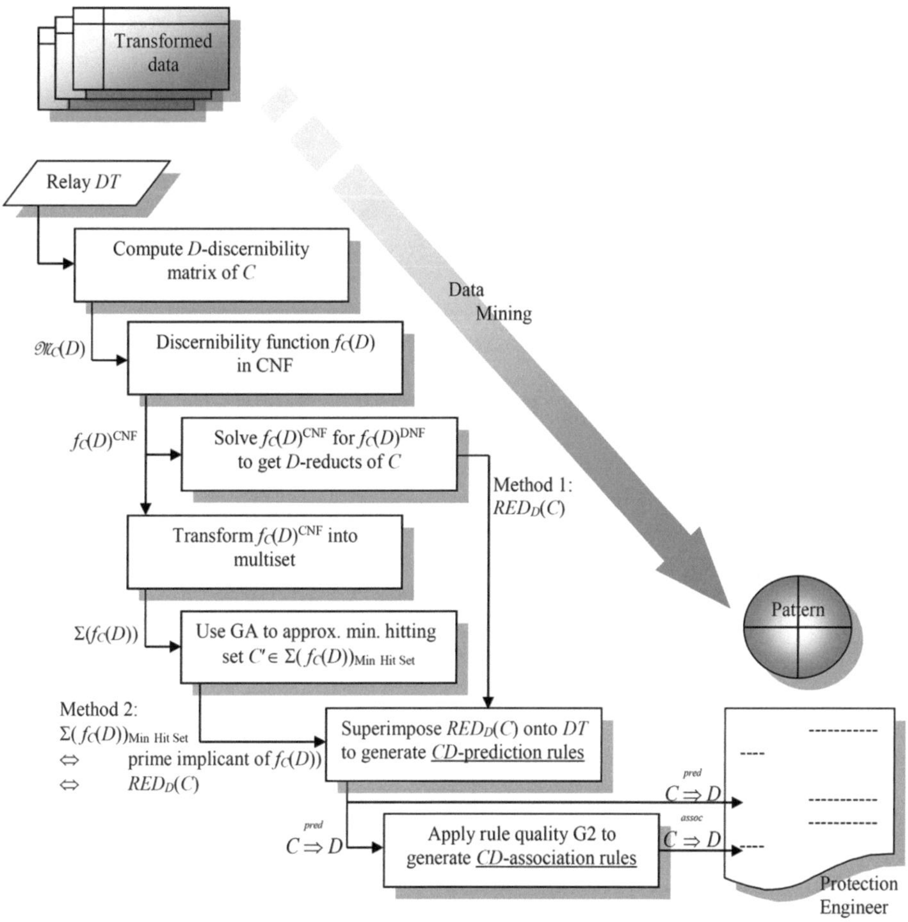

Figure 4. Data mining analysis steps in hypothesizing distance relay operation characteristics from big relay event data.

In the study, the large event report is a PSCAD-simulated raw operation recording of an AREVA-modeled distance protective relay as shown in **Table 1** (only a portion of time events is shown to reduce page usage). This big data, which is prior to data preparation, is a representation of the relay's decision system (*DS*) for zone 1 A–G fault—the so-called predata-preparation *DS* [18].

Time code	*time*	*ir*	*irp*	*vam*	*vap*	*icm*	*icp*	*CB52a_A*	*CB52a_C*	*VTmcb_C*	*VTSfail_cnfm*	*CRZ1*	*WI_CR*	*DEF_WI_CR*	*pg_Z1PkUp*	*pp_Z1PkUp*	*pp_Z4PkUp*	*AGflt*	*ABGflt*	*BCGflt*	*BCflt*	*ABC_ABCGflt*	*ab50_Z1*	*ab50_Z2*	*bc50_Z3*	*ca50_Z4*
.	.	.	.	.	.	.	.	.	.	.	.	.	.	.	.	.	.	.	.	.	.	.	.	.	.	.
.	.	.	.	.	.	.	.	.	.	.	.	.	.	.	.	.	.	.	.	.	.	.	.	.	.	.
t_{86}	*0.102*	1.090	-98.347	43.759	-43.542	0.296	90.006	1	1	0	0	0	0	0	0	0	0	1	0	0	0	0	1	1	0	0
t_{87}	*0.103*	1.177	-107.544	41.618	-47.808	0.296	89.973	1	1	0	0	0	0	0	0	0	0	1	0	0	0	0	1	1	0	0
t_{88}	*0.104*	1.209	-114.688	37.626	-52.911	0.297	90.106	1	1	0	0	0	0	0	0	0	0	1	0	0	0	0	1	1	0	0
t_{89}	*0.106*	1.206	-117.863	32.109	-56.738	0.297	90.139	1	1	0	0	0	0	0	0	0	0	1	0	0	0	0	1	1	0	0
t_{90}	*0.107*	1.209	-117.629	25.479	-57.671	0.296	90.106	1	1	0	0	0	0	0	1	0	0	1	0	0	0	0	1	1	0	0
t_{91}	*0.108*	1.266	-115.528	20.186	-53.432	0.296	90.089	1	1	0	0	0	0	0	1	0	0	1	0	0	0	0	1	1	0	0
t_{92}	*0.109*	1.387	-113.754	17.342	-43.761	0.294	90.106	1	1	0	0	0	0	0	1	0	0	1	0	0	0	0	1	1	0	0
t_{93}	*0.110*	1.537	-114.081	16.502	-35.792	0.294	90.173	1	1	0	0	0	0	0	1	0	0	1	0	0	0	0	1	1	0	0
t_{114}	*0.136*	1.689	-125.473	14.755	-48.672	0.294	90.590	1	1	0	0	0	0	0	1	0	0	1	0	0	0	0	1	1	0	0
t_{115}	*0.137*	1.682	-126.220	14.601	-48.947	0.294	90.640	1	1	0	0	0	0	0	1	0	0	1	0	0	0	0	1	1	0	0
t_{116}	*0.138*	1.673	-126.640	14.601	-48.645	0.294	90.640	1	1	0	0	0	0	0	1	0	0	1	0	0	0	0	1	1	0	0
t_{117}	*0.139*	1.659	-126.874	14.378	-47.904	0.294	90.623	1	1	0	0	0	0	0	1	0	0	1	0	0	0	0	1	1	0	0
t_{118}	*0.140*	1.643	-127.014	14.327	-47.534	0.294	90.640	1	1	0	0	0	0	0	1	0	0	1	0	0	0	0	1	1	0	0
t_{119}	*0.142*	1.631	-126.921	14.395	-46.999	0.294	90.640	1	1	0	0	0	0	0	1	0	0	1	0	0	0	0	1	1	0	0
t_{120}	*0.143*	1.619	-126.640	14.429	-45.888	0.294	90.606	1	1	0	0	0	0	0	1	0	0	1	0	0	0	0	1	1	0	0
t_{121}	*0.144*	1.612	-126.314	14.515	-45.970	0.294	90.640	1	1	0	0	0	0	0	1	0	0	1	0	0	0	0	1	1	0	0
t_{122}	*0.145*	1.611	-125.987	14.738	-45.435	0.294	90.690	1	1	0	0	0	0	0	1	0	0	1	0	0	0	0	1	1	0	0
t_{123}	*0.146*	1.612	-125.520	14.909	-45.462	0.294	90.673	1	1	0	0	0	0	0	1	0	0	1	0	0	0	0	1	1	0	0
t_{124}	*0.148*	1.617	-125.333	15.012	-45.696	0.294	90.673	1	1	0	0	0	0	0	1	0	0	1	0	0	0	0	1	1	0	0
t_{125}	*0.149*	1.624	-125.100	15.252	-46.340	0.294	90.673	1	1	0	0	0	0	0	1	0	0	1	0	0	0	0	1	1	0	0
t_{126}	*0.150*	1.632	-125.006	15.252	-46.628	0.294	90.673	1	1	0	0	0	0	0	1	0	0	1	0	0	0	0	1	1	0	0
.	.	.	.	.	.	.	.	.	.	.	.	.	.	.	.	.	.	.	.	.	.	.	.	.	.	.
.	.	.	.	.	.	.	.	.	.	.	.	.	.	.	.	.	.	.	.	.	.	.	.	.	.	.

(Continued)

(A total of 108 attributes. Only some are shown)

(Continued)

b50_Z1	*c50_Z2*	*c50_Z4*	*r50_Z1*	*PSB_Z1pp*	*PSB_Z4pp*	*QF32*	*Zload_fwd*	*Q50_1*	*Dist_ab_Z1*	*Dist_ab_Z2*	*Dist_bc_Z4*	*Dist_cg_Z3*	*Dist_cg_Z4*	*pg_TrpZ1f*	*pp_TrpZ1f*	*TrpPUPZ2*	*TrpPOPZ1*	*WI_TrpA*	*WI_CRTrp*	*DEFelem1_trp*	*TrpBOP_DEF*	*DEF_WI_TrpA*	*Trip_PhA*	*Trip_PhB*	*Trip_PhC*
.	.	.	.	.	.	.	.	.	.	.	.	.	.	.	.	.	.	.	.	.	.	.	.	.	.
0	0	0	1	0	0	1	1	1	0	0	0	0	0	0	0	0	0	0	0	0	0	0	0	0	0
0	0	0	1	0	0	1	1	1	0	0	0	0	0	0	0	0	0	0	0	0	0	0	0	0	0
0	0	0	1	0	0	1	0	1	0	0	0	0	0	0	0	0	0	0	0	0	0	0	0	0	0
0	0	0	1	0	0	1	0	1	0	0	0	0	0	0	0	0	0	0	0	0	0	0	0	0	0
0	0	0	1	0	0	1	0	1	0	0	0	0	0	1	0	0	0	0	0	0	0	0	0	0	0
0	0	0	1	0	0	1	0	1	0	0	0	0	0	1	0	0	0	0	0	0	0	0	1	0	0
0	0	0	1	0	0	1	0	1	0	0	0	0	0	1	0	0	0	0	0	0	0	0	1	0	0
0	0	0	1	0	0	1	0	1	0	0	0	0	0	1	0	0	0	0	0	0	0	0	1	0	0
0	0	0	1	0	0	1	0	1	0	0	0	0	0	1	0	0	0	0	0	0	0	0	1	0	0
0	0	0	1	0	0	1	0	1	0	0	0	0	0	1	0	0	0	0	0	0	0	0	1	0	0
0	0	0	1	0	0	1	0	1	0	0	0	0	0	1	0	0	0	0	0	0	0	0	1	0	0
0	0	0	1	0	0	1	0	1	0	0	0	0	0	1	0	0	0	0	0	0	0	0	1	0	0
0	0	0	1	0	0	1	0	1	0	0	0	0	0	1	0	0	0	0	0	0	0	0	1	0	0
0	0	0	1	0	0	1	0	1	0	0	0	0	0	1	0	0	0	0	0	0	0	0	1	0	0
0	0	0	1	0	0	1	0	1	0	0	0	0	0	1	0	0	0	0	0	0	0	0	1	0	0
0	0	0	1	0	0	1	0	1	0	0	0	0	0	1	0	0	0	0	0	0	0	0	1	0	0
0	0	0	1	0	0	1	0	1	0	0	0	0	0	1	0	0	0	0	0	0	0	0	1	0	0
0	0	0	1	0	0	1	0	1	0	0	0	0	0	1	0	0	0	0	0	0	0	0	1	0	0
0	0	0	1	0	0	1	0	1	0	0	0	0	0	1	0	0	0	0	0	0	0	0	1	0	0
0	0	0	1	0	0	1	0	1	0	0	0	0	0	1	0	0	0	0	0	0	0	0	1	0	0
0	0	0	1	0	0	1	0	1	0	0	0	0	0	1	0	0	0	0	0	0	0	0	1	0	0
.	.	.	.	.	.	.	.	.	.	.	.	.	.	.	.	.	.	.	.	.	.	.	.	.	.
.	.	.	.	.	.	.	.	.	.	.	.	.	.	.	.	.	.	.	.	.	.	.	.	.	.

Table 1. Predata-preparation of distance protective relay's decision system for zone 1 A-G fault (only a portion of attribute columns (from a total of 108) and time events are shown to reduce page usage).

The decision system is an information table of event report that can be considered as a pair of finite and nonempty set (*U*, *A*). *U* is the universe of objects (i.e., time tagged relay events t_n, thus called event report) and A is the set of attributes {e.g., *ir, irp, vam, iam, ibm, icm, CB52a_B, CB52b_B, VTmcb_B, CRZ4, pg_Z3PkUp, pg_Z4PkUp, pp_Z1PkUp, pp_Z2PkUp, AGflt, c50_Z1, b50_Z3, Dist_ab_Z2, pg_TrpZ1f, TrpBOPZ1, WI_CRTrp, Trip_PhA*, etc.}. Each attribute $a \in A$ defines an information function such that, f_a: $U \rightarrow V_a$, where V_a is the set of values of the attribute a, called the domain of a. For instance, the set of values of the attribute *pg_Z1PkUp* (the "zone 1 ground distance pick-up" element) is expressed as *pg_Z1PkUp*: $U \rightarrow \{0, 1\}$, which defines the relay element's active states according to the presence of ground fault in the protected section of transmission line (i.e., no-fault present or zone-1-ground-fault present).

Time code	*time*	*Zab*	*Zbc*	*Zca*	*Zag*	*Zbg*	*Zcg*	*CB52_A*	*CB52_B*	*CB52_C*	*VTmcb*	*VTSfail_cnfm*	*CR*	*pg_PkUp*	*pp_PkUp*	*FltType*	*pp50_Z1*	*pp50_Z2*	*pp50_Z3*	*pp50_Z4*	*p50_Z1*	*p50_Z2*	*p50_Z3*	*p50_Z4*	*r50*	*PSB*	*Q32*	*Zload*	*Q50*	*Dist_ab*	*Dist_bc*	*Dist_ca*	*Dist_ag*	*Dist_bg*	*Dist_cg*	*pg_Trp*	*pp_Trp*	*Trip_CAPerm*	*Trip_CABlck*	*WI_Trp*	*WI_CRTrp*	*DEFelem_Trp*	*DEF_WI_CRTrp*	*Trip_DEF_CA*	*DEF_WI_Trp*	*Trip*
t_{76}	0.090	0	0	0	0	0	0	closed	closed	closed	0	0	0	0	0	no fault	0	0	0	0	0	0	0	0	0	0	Fwd	Fwd	0	0	0	0	0	0	0	0	0	0	0	0	0	0	0	0	0	0
t_{77}	0.091	0	0	0	0	0	0	closed	closed	closed	0	0	0	0	0	no fault	0	0	0	0	0	0	0	0	0	0	Fwd	Fwd	0	0	0													0	0	0
t_{78}	0.092	0	0	0	0	0	0	closed	closed	closed	0	0	0	0	0	no fault	0	0	0	0	0	0	0	0	0	0	Fwd	Fwd	0	0	0													0	0	0
t_{79}	0.094	0	0	0	0	0	0	closed	closed	closed	0	0	0	0	0	no fault	0	0	0	0	0	0	0	0	0	0	Fwd	Fwd	0	0	0													0	0	0
t_{80}	0.095	0	0	0	0	0	0	closed	closed	closed	0	0	0	0	0	no fault	0	0	0	A	0	A	A	A	0	0	Fwd	Fwd	0	0	0													0	0	0
t_{81}	0.096	0	0	0	0	0	0	closed	closed	closed	0	0	0	0	0	no fault	0	A	A	A	A	A	A	A	0	0	Fwd	Fwd	0	0	0													0	0	0
t_{82}	0.097	0	0	0	0	0	0	closed	closed	closed	0	0	0	0	0	AGflt	A	A	A	A	A	A	A	A	34	0	Fwd	Fwd	4	0	0													0	0	0
t_{83}	0.098	0	0	0	0	0	0	closed	closed	closed	0	0	0	0	0	AGflt	A	A	A	A	A	A	A	A	234	0	Fwd	Fwd	4	0	0													0	0	0
t_{84}	0.100	0	0	0	0	0	0	closed	closed	closed	0	0	0	0	0	AGflt	A	A	A	A	A	A	A	A	1234	0	Fwd	Fwd	1234	0	0													0	0	0
t_{85}	0.101	0	0	0	0	0	0	closed	closed	closed	0	0	0	0	0	AGflt	A	A	A	A	A	A	A	A	1234	0	Fwd	Fwd	1234	0	0													0	0	0
t_{86}	0.102	0	0	0	3	0	0	closed	closed	closed	0	0	0	23	0	AGflt	A	A	A	A	A	A	A	A	1234	0	Fwd	Fwd	1234	0	0													0	0	0
t_{87}	0.103	0	0	0	23	0	0	closed	closed	closed	0	0	0	23	0	AGflt	A	A	A	A	A	A	A	A	1234	0	Fwd	Fwd	1234	0	0													0	0	0
t_{88}	0.104	0	0	0	23	0	0	closed	closed	closed	0	0	0	23	0	AGflt	A	A	A	A	A	A	A	A	1234	0	Fwd	0	1234	0	0	0	23	0	0	0	0	0	0	0			0	0	0	0
t_{89}	0.106	0	0	0	23	0	0	closed	closed	closed	0	0	0	23	0	AGflt	A	A	A	A	A	A	A	A	1234	0	Fwd	0	1234	0	0	0	23	0	0	0	0	0	0	0	0	0	0		0	0
t_{90}	0.107	0	0	0	123	0	0	closed	closed	closed	0	0	0	123	0	AGflt	A	A	A	A	A	A	A	A	1234	0	Fwd	0	1234	0	0	0	123	0	0	1	0	0	0	0	0	0	0	0	0	0
t_{91}	0.108	0	0	0	123	0	0	closed	closed	closed	0	0	0	123	0	AGflt	A	A	A	A	A	A	A	A	1234	0	Fwd	0	1234	0	0	0	123	0	0	1	0	0	0	0	0	0	0	0	0	A
.	.	.	.	.	.	.	.	.	.	.	.	.	.	.	.	.	.	.	.	.	.	.	.	.	.	.	.	.	.	.	.	.	.	.	.	.	.	.	.	.	.	.	.	.	.	.
t_{128}	0.152	0	0	0	123	0	0	closed	closed	closed	0	0	0	123	0	AGflt	A	A	A	A	A	A	A	A	1234	0	Fwd	0	1234	0	0	0	123	0	0	1	0	0	0	0	0	0	0	0	0	A
t_{129}	0.154	0	0	0	123	0	0	open	closed	closed	0	0	0	123	0	no fault	A	A	A	A	A	A	A	A	1234	0	Fwd	0	1234	0	0	0	0	0	0	0	0	0	0	0	0	0	0	0	0	A
.	.	.	.	.	.	.	.	.	.	.	.	.	.	.	.	.	.	.	.	.	.	.	.	.	.	.	.	.	.	.	.	.	.	.	.	.	.	.	.	.	.	.	.	.	.	.
t_{140}	0.167	0	0	0	123	0	0	open	closed	closed	0	0	0	123	0	no fault	A	A	A	A	A	A	A	A	1234	0	Fwd	0	1234	0	0	0	0	0	0	0	0	0	0	0	0	0	0	0	0	A
t_{141}	0.168	0	0	0	123	0	0	open	closed	closed	0	0	0	123	0	no fault	A	A	A	A	A	AB	AB	AB	1234	0	Fwd	0	1234	0	0	0	0	0	0	0	0	0	0	0	0	0	0	0	0	A
t_{142}	0.169	0	0	0	123	0	0	open	closed	closed	0	0	0	123	0	no fault	A	A	A	AB	A	AB	AB	AB	1234	0	Fwd	0	1234	0	0	0	0	0	0	0	0	0	0	0	0	0	0	0	0	A
t_{143}	0.170	0	0	0	123	0	0	open	closed	closed	0	0	0	123	0	no fault	A	A	A	AB	A	AB	AB	AB	1234	0	Fwd	0	1234	0	0	0	0	0	0	0	0	0	0	0	0	0	0	0	0	A
t_{144}	0.172	0	0	0	123	0	0	open	closed	closed	0	0	0	123	0	no fault	A	A	A	AB	AB	AB	AB	AB	1234	0	Fwd	0	1234	0	0	0	0	0	0	0	0	0	0	0	0	0	0	0	0	A
t_{145}	0.173	0	0	0	123	0	0	open	closed	closed	0	0	0	123	0	no fault	A	A	A	AB	AB	AB	AB	AB	1234	0	Fwd	0	1234	0	0	0	0	0	0	0	0	0	0	0	0	0	0	0	0	A
t_{146}	0.174	0	0	0	123	0	0	open	closed	closed	0	0	0	123	0	no fault	A	A	AB	AB	AB	AB	AB	AB	1234	0	Fwd	Fwd	1234	0	0	0	0	0	0	0	0	0	0	0	0	0	0	0	0	A
t_{147}	0.175	0	0	0	123	0	0	open	closed	closed	0	0	0	123	0	no fault	A	A	AB	AB	AB	AB	AB	AB	1234	0	Fwd	Fwd	1234	0	0	0	0	0	0	0	0	0	0	0	0	0	0	0	0	A
t_{148}	0.176	0	0	0	123	0	0	open	closed	closed	0	0	0	123	0	no fault	A	A	AB	AB	AB	AB	AB	AB	1234	0	Fwd	Fwd	1234	0	0	0	0	0	0	0	0	0	0	0	0	0	0	0	0	A
t_{149}	0.178	0	0	0	123	0	0	open	closed	closed	0	0	0	123	0	no fault	A	A	AB	AB	AB	AB	AB	AB	1234	0	Fwd	0	1234	0	0	0	0	0	0	0	0	0	0	0	0	0	0	0	0	A
t_{150}	0.179	0	0	0	123	0	0	open	closed	closed	0	0	0	123	0	no fault	A	A	AB	AB	AB	AB	AB	AB	1234	0	Fwd	0	1234	0	0	0	0	0	0	0	0	0	0	0	0	0	0	0	0	A
t_{151}	0.180	0	0	0	123	0	0	open	closed	closed	0	0	0	123	0	no fault	A	AB	AB	AB	AB	AB	AB	AB	1234	0	Fwd	Fwd	1234	0	0	0	0	0	0	0	0	0	0	0	0	0	0	0	0	A
t_{152}	0.181	0	0	0	123	0	0	open	closed	closed	0	0	0	123	0	no fault	0	B	B	B	B	AB	AB	AB	1234	0	Fwd	Fwd	4	0	0	0	0	0	0	0	0	0	0	0	0	0	0	0	0	A
t_{153}	0.182	0	0	0	123	0	0	open	closed	closed	0	0	0	123	0	no fault	C	B	B	B	B	B	B	B	1234	0	Fwd	0	4	0	0	0	0	0	0	0	0	0	0	0	0	0	0	0	0	A
t_{154}	0.184	0	0	0	123	0	0	open	closed	closed	0	0	0	123	0	no fault	C	B	B	B	B	B	B	B	1234	0	Rev	0	4	0	0	0	0	0	0	0	0	0	0	0	0	0	0	0	0	A
.	.	.	.	.	.	.	.	.	.	.	.	.	.	.	.	.	.	.	.	.	.	.	.	.	.	.	.	.	.	.	.	.	.	.	.	.	.	.	.	.	.	.	.	.	.	.
t_{169}	0.202	0	0	0	0	0	0	open	closed	closed	0	0	0	0	0	no fault	0	0	B	B	B	B	B	B	34	0	Rev	0	4	0	0	0	0	0	0	0	0	0	0	0	0	0	0	0	0	A
t_{170}	0.203	0	0	0	0	0	0	open	closed	closed	0	0	0	0	0	no fault	0	0	B	B	B	B	B	B	34	0	Rev	0	4	0	0	0	0	0	0	0	0	0	0	0	0	0	0	0	0	A
t_{171}	0.204	0	0	0	0	0	0	open	closed	closed	0	0	0	0	0	no fault	0	0	0	B	B	B	B	B	34	0	Rev	0	4	0	0	0	0	0	0	0	0	0	0	0	0	0	0	0	0	A
.	.	.	.	.	.	.	.	.	.	.	.	.	.	.	.	.	.	.	.	.	.	.	.	.	.	.	.	.	.	.	.	.	.	.	.	.	.	.	.	.	.	.	.	.	.	.
t_{175}	0.209	0	0	0	0	0	0	open	closed	closed	0	0	0	0	0	no fault	0	0	0	B	B	B	B	B	34	0	Rev	0	4	0	0	0	0	0	0	0	0	0	0	0	0	0	0	0	0	A
t_{176}	0.210	0	0	0	0	0	0	open	closed	closed	0	0	0	0	0	no fault	0	0	0	B	0	B	B	B	34	0	Rev	0	4	0	0	0	0	0	0	0	0	0	0	0	0	0	0	0	0	A
t_{177}	0.211	0	0	0	0	0	0	open	closed	closed	0	0	0	0	0	no fault	0	0	0	B	0	B	B	B	4	0	Rev	Fwd	4	0	0	0	0	0	0	0	0	0	0	0	0	0	0	0	0	A
t_{178}	0.212	0	0	0	0	0	0	open	closed	closed	0	0	0	0	0	no fault	0	0	0	0	0	0	0	0	0	0	Rev	Fwd	4	0	0	0	0	0	0	0	0	0	0	0	0	0	0	0	0	A
.	.	.	.	.	.	.	.	.	.	.	.	.	.	.	.	.	.	.	.	.	.	.	.	.	.	.	.	.	.	.	.	.	.	.	.	.	.	.	.	.	.	.	.	.	.	.
t_{278}	0.333	0	0	0	0	0	0	open	closed	closed	0	0	0	0	0	no fault	0	0	0	0	0	0	0	0	0	0	Rev	Fwd	4	0	0	0	0	0	0	0	0	0	0	0	0	0	0	0	0	A
t_{279}	0.334	0	0	0	0	0	0	open	closed	closed	0	0	0	0	0	no fault	0	0	0	0	0	0	0	0	0	0	Rev	Fwd	4	0	0	0	0	0	0	0	0	0	0	0	0	0	0	0	0	0
.	.	.	.	.	.	.	.	.	.	.	.	.	.	.	.	.	.	.	.	.	.	.	.	.	.	.	.	.	.	.	.	.	.	.	.	.	.	.	.	.	.	.	.	.	.	.
.	.	.	.	.	.	.	.	.	.	.	.	.	.	.	.	.	.	.	.	.	.	.	.	.	.	.	.	.	.	.	.	.	.	.	.	.	.	.	.	.	.	.	.	.	.	.
t_{320}	0.383	0	0	0	0	0	0	open	closed	closed	0	0	0	0	0	no fault	0	0	0	0	0	0	0	0	0	0	Fwd	Fwd	0	0	0	0	0	0	0	0	0	0	0	0	0	0	0	0	0	0
t_{321}	0.384	0	0	0	0	0	0	closed	closed	closed	0	0	0	0	0	no fault	0	0	0	0	0	0	0	0	0	0	Fwd	Fwd	0	0	0	0	0	0	0	0	0	0	0	0	0	0	0	0	0	0
t_{322}	0.385	0	0	0	0	0	0	closed	closed	closed	0	0	0	0	0	no fault	0	0	0	0	0	0	0	0	0	0	Fwd	Fwd	0	0	0	0	0	0	0	0	0	0	0	0	0	0	0	0	0	0
t_{323}	0.387	0	0	0	0	0	0	closed	closed	closed	0	0	0	0	0	no fault	0	0	0	0	0	0	0	0	0	0	Fwd	Fwd	0	0	0	0	0	0	0	0	0	0	0	0	0	0	0	0	0	0
t_{324}	0.388	0	0	0	0	0	0	closed	closed	closed	0	0	0	0	0	no fault	0	0	0	0	0	0	0	0	0	0	Fwd	Fwd	0	0	0	0	0	0	0	0	0	0	0	0	0	0	0	0	0	0

Inconsistent decision patterns between these events (i.e., similar condition attributes but the decision attribute *Trip* goes from 0 to A) that can be immediately recognized to have association with tripping signal assertion for CB.

Table 2. The predata-mining *DS* of distance protective relay subjected to zone 1 A-G fault.

Here, A is $A = C \cup D$ which is a nonempty finite union set of condition and decision attributes (condition attributes $c_i \subset C$ suggest the multifunctional protective elements and analog measurands while decision attribute $d_i \subset D$ suggests the relay's trip output).

This big data is a hindrance in a laborious manual extraction of relay operation characteristics for the Expert System development. Thus, the aforementioned novel integrated data mining strategy is necessary to address this issue.

The resulting prepared decision table (after data selection, preprocessing, and transformation) of the distance protective relay's decision system is shown in **Table 2**. It is also called postdata-preparation *DS* or predata-mining *DS*. "." denotes data patterns that are similar to events immediately before and after them. Thus, they are not presented in order to reduce the table dimension. It is noticeable that the number of attributes has been substantially reduced by the data preparation strategy to merely 46 from the original 108 in the large raw event report.

The important analysis steps in the framework of Rough Set based data mining for deriving the distance relay decision algorithm from its event database is illustrated in **Figure 4** and discussed herewith.

The *computation of reducts* which is a process of reducing the number attributes while still maintaining the original data syntax is performed to start with. Within this the following substeps are executed:

a. Computation of the D-discernibility matrix of C (denoted as $\mathcal{M}_C(D)$). An element of $\mathcal{M}_C(D)$ is defined as the set of all condition attributes which discern events t_i and t_j and do not belong to the same equivalence class of the relation $U|IND(D)$.

b. Subsequent derivation of the discernibility function $f_C(D)$ in Conjunctive Normal Form (CNF) (also called POS form in Boolean algebra) from $M_C(D)$. The CNF is reduced to final form after absorption law and omission of duplicates of disjunctive terms (sums) are applied minus the multiplication among each of the disjunctive terms of the final CNF.

c. In empirical database such as in this relay event data analysis, the calculation toward arriving at the final Disjunctive Normal Form (DNF) in order to find the eventual reducts is extremely computationally intensive. (DNF is obtained if the multiplication among each of the disjunctive terms of the final CNF is performed). In this case, the generation of reducts is considered as an NP-hard problem [19]. Thus, Genetic Algorithm is adopted to compute approximations of reducts by finding the minimally approximate hitting sets (analogous to reducts) from the sets corresponding to the discernibility function [20, 21].

Next *prediction rules* (denoted as $C \overset{pred}{\Longrightarrow} D$) are generated in which the above discovered reducts serve as the templates for the prediction rules to be created from. This is principally done by superimposing each reduct in the reduct set over the original decision table *DS* and then reading off the domain values of the condition and decision attributes. The resulting logical patterns, denoted as $C \Rightarrow D$), that relate descriptions of condition to decision classes shall have the representation shown in Eq. (**1**):

$$C \overset{pred}{\Rightarrow} D : \text{IF } c_i = v_{c_i} \text{AND} \ldots \text{AND} \, c_k = v_{c_k} \text{THEN} \, Trip = v_{Trip} \quad (1)$$

These prediction rules that are an exact representation of the characteristics of the relay decision system (table) *DS* can be described as the relay decision algorithm and can be designated as *ALG*(*DS*), i.e.,

$$ALG(DS) = \bigcup_{t \in \cup} (C \overset{pred}{\Rightarrow} D)_t \quad (2)$$

where $(C \overset{pred}{\Rightarrow} D)_t$ is the set of minimal prediction rules $C \overset{pred}{\Rightarrow} D$ for an event $t \in \cup$, i.e.,

$$(C \overset{pred}{\Rightarrow} D)_t : \text{IF } c_i = v_{c_i}(t) \text{AND} \ldots \text{AND} \, c_k = v_{c_k}(t) \text{THEN} \, Trip = v_{Trip}(t) \quad (3)$$

This *ALG*(*DS*) can be evaluated for its accuracy as follows:

a. The entire original relay data set *DS* is partitioned into training and test sets using k-fold cross validation technique.

b. Estimating classification performance of the relay decision algorithm by rule firing-voting strategies.

The discovered *ALG*(*DS*) has been evaluated and verified by Othman et al. [15–17] to be able to be used to predict and discriminate future relay events having unknown trip state in unsupervised learning. This evaluation is necessary prior to allowing the eventual deduction of the relay association rule to take place.

Finally, postpruning (or filtering) is performed on the generated prediction rules $(C \overset{pred}{\Rightarrow} D)$ so as to discover relay *association rules* (denoted as $C \overset{pred}{\Rightarrow} D$). These pertinent association rules essentially characterize the tripping decision logic of protective relay upon fault detection. This has been referred at the outset as the hypothesization of protective relay operation. This final version of knowledge representation shall be the main constituent for the Expert System knowledge base.

Because there are too large prediction rules to be filtered from, it is difficult to manually determine which rules are more useful, interesting, or important. Therefore, a measure of rule quality called *G2 Likelihood Ratio Statistic* as well as a measure of rule interestingness are used to select the most appropriate relay association rules and filter away the unwanted ones.

As mentioned above, these finally discovered relay association rules essentially describe the logical pattern of the correlating descriptions of conditions (i.e., *C*, the attribute set for various multifunctional protection elements) and the decision class (i.e., *D*, the attribute for trip assertion status). Thus, the symbol *CD* is used to illustrate *C-D* association and "*CD-association rule*" has been labeled as such to recognize it.

The final *CD*-association rule for one such fault condition as zone 1 A–G fault is shown in Eq. (**4**). Different fault condition would provide correspondingly different association rules to describe the relay's behavior.

$$\begin{array}{l}\textbf{IF}\ Zag(123)\,\text{AND}\ CB52\_A(\text{closed})\,\text{AND}\ pg\_PkUp(123)\\ \text{AND}\ FltType(\text{AGflt})\,\text{AND}\ pp50\_Z3(\text{A})\\ \text{AND}\ pp50\_Z4(\text{A})\,\text{AND}\ p50\_Z1(\text{A})\,\text{AND}\\ \text{p50\_Z3(A)}\,\text{AND}\ r50(1234)\,\text{AND}\ Q32(\text{Fwd})\,\text{AND}\\ Zload(0)\,\text{AND}\ Q50(1234)\,\text{AND}\ Dist\_ag(123)\,\text{AND}\ pg\_Trp(1)\ \textbf{THEN}\ Trip(\text{A})\end{array} \tag{4}$$

It is important to note that Eq. (**4**) defines the necessary triggering of the required relay multifunctional protective elements (antecedent) in order to recognize the zone 1 phase-A-to-ground fault and consequently assert the trip signal (consequent) to open pole A of the circuit breaker concerned. This is what the protection engineers would like to know in understanding the domain of the distance relay in responding to the fault.

Thus, it is necessary to verify how true it is that this rule can be used to interpret the distance relay behavior subjected to zone 1 A–G fault as represented by the predata-mining *DS* in Table 2. Out of all the relay events in the entire length of the relay event report, relay events $t_{90}$and t_{91} identified as the *fault detection* and *trip signal assertion* instances, respectively, will be our emphasis for cross reference to verify the exactness of the above-mentioned rationalized *CD*-association rule. In Table 2, the rule is seen to be an exact interpretation of the relay events $t_{90}$and t_{91}. Thus, the discovered rationalized *CD*-association rule is verified.

The eventually discovered ($C \overset{assoc}{\Rightarrow} D$), and thus the desired hypothesis, has been proven to be an exact manifestation of the relay operation characteristics hidden in the event report [15–17]. The intelligent data mining framework provides the potential facility to conveniently discover exhaustively available knowledge of relay behavior from big event data subjected to exhaustively possible fault contingencies. Ultimately, a complete rule base for inference execution of an Expert System for relay operation analysis can be developed. This is the motivation of developing an Expert System called Protective Relay Analysis System (PRAY) that provides a platform for gathering previously discovered rules for its knowledge base construction.

3. Developing protective relay analysis system (PRAY) expert system

The concept of protective relay performance analysis is related to the convention that in any analysis known or correct events must first be hypothesized (expected operations are assumed), then an analysis is performed to confirm (validate) or refute the hypothesis by running matching exercise between expected and actual operations of the device under test [22]. If it is determined that the protective relay operation was incorrect, the diagnosis for cause must be performed [8]. This fundamental concept shall form the very basis of developing PRAY for distance protection.

PRAY is developed as an application tool under LabVIEW framework from National Instruments [23]. The main components of PRAY are as shown in **Figure 5** and described as follows:

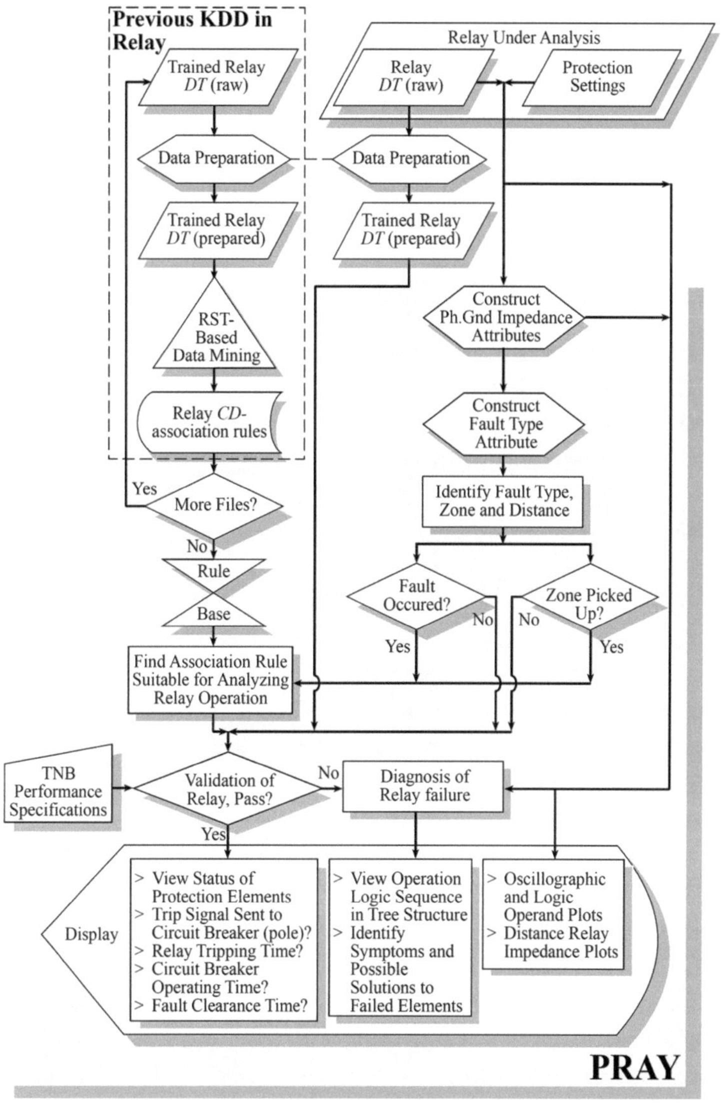

Figure 5. Architecture of Protective Relay Analysis System (PRAY).

i. Construction of a rule base for PRAY's inference engine by collating as an array all relay *CD*-association rules discovered from the KDD processes performed on trained relay. All attributes of each rule in the rule base shall be time tagged and arranged in a chronological order so that validation and diagnosis of the analyzed relay's operations can be presented in an apparent operations logical sequence.

ii. Construction of phase and ground distance impedance channels (attributes) and fault-type channel. Using these channels, further identification processes of fault type, faulted zone, and distance to fault are executed and later used in singling out the most suitable relay *CD*-association rule from the rule base.

iii. Inferring, from the rule base according to both impending fault type and zone of pick-up, an expected relay *CD*-association rule to be best chosen as a hypothesis for the prediction of operations logic of the relay under analysis.

iv. Validation of occurrence of protective element pick-ups and their correctness of operations against hypothesis of the selected relay *CD*-association rule.

v. Symptom of relay element misoperation and its diagnosis as well as possible solution suggestion.

vi. Graphical plots of ground and phase impedance locus against respective ground and phase distance quadrilateral characteristics. The distance characteristics are constructed based on parameter settings taken from the relay under analysis. Instantaneous filtered voltages and currents and logic operands are also plotted.

3.1. PRAY inputs

The different inputs needed by PRAY for its analysis functions are as follows:

i. Relay *CD*-association rules: These rules saved as a plain text format in the KDD process are collated via graphical user interface (GUI) dialog input. The user is prompted for sufficient number of rules to be imported. The collated rules are converted into an array to form a rule base for the Expert System inference engine. Each rule input is an outcome of KDD after the Rough-Set-and-Genetic-Algorithm-based data mining and Rule Quality Measure (*G2* Likelihood Ratio Statistic) in ROSETTA [24]. In its untreated form, each rule input consists of a number of sub-*CD*-association rules. These subrules are rationalized into a single $C \Rightarrow D$ form by taking conjunction of them and using the concept of Boolean function manipulation by applying law of absorption.

ii. Analyzed relay event reports in the form of raw and prepared decision systems, (relay *DSs*): The raw relay *DS* is a converted data from relay resident IEEE COMTRADE format to DIAdem native format (.tdm), which is needed for processing in LabVIEW [25]. The prepared relay *DS* is a resultant file after the same data preparation process as that in the KDD for trained relay. This prepared relay *DS* in DIAdem format (.tdm) is of the same data structure as that used in the KDD; the latter is ready for the Rough Set data mining albeit not executed on for the expert system analysis. Having the same data structure is important so that the prepared *DS* of the relay under analysis can be correctly cross validated with a *CD*-association rule chosen from the PRAY rule base.

iii. Protection parameter settings: Imbedded as a separate "channel group" from the raw relay *DS*'s channel group in the same tdm file. The relay settings are originally recorded by the relay under analysis as a number of COMTRADE files. Since they are in the same file as the raw relay *DS*, they are also converted by DIAdem into tdm format.

iv. Performance specifications: The user has the option to key in values for parameters. For simplicity of analysis, TNB specifications for relay tripping time according to various zones of protection have been included as default values without requiring user's inputs. (TNB is a short form for Tenaga Nasional Berhad, a Malaysian major utility organization.)

3.2. PRAY reasoning strategy for validation and diagnosis

The reasoning for validation and diagnosis of relay operations analysis starts with identification of fault type, faulted zone, and distance to fault by PRAY itself. The information from the fault type and picked-up faulted zone is then used to determine the index in the rule base array to determine the subarray containing the appropriate relay *CD*-association rule to be used in analyzing the relay under analysis. This chosen rule shall act as the hypothesis of anticipated operations of individual protective elements in the relay under analysis when a particular fault has occurred. All the antecedents and consequent in the rule have been initially arranged in sequential order during the rule base construction according to the time instances that have been tagged alongside them. Time tagging is important so that validation and diagnosis of relay operations can be executed according to the logical sequence stipulated by the hypothesis. This logical sequence is in fact indicative of relay operations logic. The following is a fictitious example of relay operation hypothesis based on a chosen relay *CD*-association rule:

0.000 *CB52_B*(closed) *Q32*(Fwd)

0.096 *p50_Z1*(B)

0.097 *FltType*(BGflt)

0.100 *Q50*(1234) *r50*(1234)

0.104 *Zload*(0)

0.107 *Dist_bg*(123) *Zbg*(123) *pg_PkUp*(123) *pg_Trp*(1)

0.108 *Trip*(B)

The consequent *Trip*(B) is associated with antecedents occurring beforehand. Any protective elements (antecedents) on the same row having the same time tagging indicate that they pick up (or stay in certain states) in concurrence. Expectedly, the last row having the highest tagged time must be the consequent (decision attribute) *Trip*(B).

The validation strategy of the operations of the analyzed relay starts by iterating through all antecedents in the hypothesis and comparing each one with that of the corresponding attribute of the prepared *DS* of the relay under analysis. Matched values result in messages describing the correctness of operations of the respective protective elements. On the other hand, any differences in the cross matches (either due to wrong pick-up values or nonassertion of the respective protective elements) will produce messages describing the relay's failed elements. The result of the validation is presented starting from the consequent (decision attribute, "*Trip*") at the top followed by antecedents arranged in descending sequence according to the order of the time tags in the hypothesis.

Diagnosis is carried out on failed, inoperative or misoperative protective elements. To view the cause–effect of events, a hierarchical tree is constructed based on the hypothesis where nodes are all hierarchically time sequenced, increasing in time from downstream nodes toward root node. The root node (top most) is the consequent of all the downstream antecedent nodes. Antecedents at the same nodes (i.e., having the same indentation) are concurrent in time instance. For the above-mentioned hypothesis, the diagnosis shall follow the following hierarchy:

Trip(B)
- *Dist_bg*(123)
- *Zbg*(123)
- *pg_PkUp*(123)
- *pg_Trp*(1)
  - *Zload*(0)
    - *Q50*(1234)
    - *r50*(1234)
      - *FltType*(BGflt)
        - *p50_Z1*(B)
          - *CB52_B*(closed)
          - *Q32*(Fwd)

4. PRAY analysis system results

In the rule base construction of PRAY, each of the imported *CD*-association rules, prior to being rationalized using the concept of Boolean function manipulation by applying the law of

http://dx.doi.org/10.5772/63756

absorption, would be formatted by ROSETTA into a text file. When imported into PRAY, the file will be cleared of all unnecessary data such as comments and rule interestingness numerical measures leaving only the required relay *CD*-association rules for subsequent rationalization.

Figure 6 illustrates the GUI for the constructed rule base. Size of rule base and the selected subarray (0-indexed) of collated rule base array are shown. The size of the rule base reflects the number of training of various fault contingencies the trained relay has been subjected to.

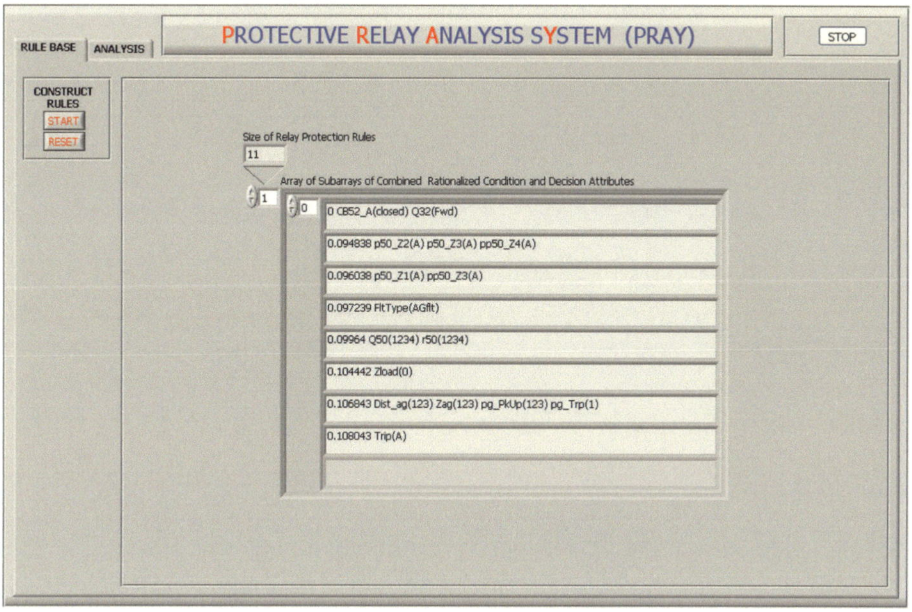

Figure 6. GUI for constructed rule base.

Figure 7 illustrates the GUI for analysis of a distance protective relay operation that has been subjected to a zone-1-AG fault. Using data in the relay's raw tdm file, PRAY discovered that an AG fault has indeed occurred in zone 1 of the relay under analysis at approximately 39 km from its location in the substation. From this information, an appropriate relay *CD*-association rule has been chosen and displayed in the GUI. This rule shall be used to analyze whether any appropriate measures have been taken by the relay under analysis to clear the fault. In validating the individual operations of protective elements, the Validation field displays the correctness of actions taken by the relay after cross matching anticipated operations of individual protective elements hypothesized by the rule with the corresponding attributes obtained from the preprocessed tdm relay file under analysis. The consequent "Trip" is validated to have correctly sent a pole A trip signal to the circuit breaker. This is followed by correct antecedent statuses arranged in descending sequence according to the hypothesis. The relay tripping time of 1.2 ms is compliant with the TNB requirement of 25 ms for zone 1 operation. The circuit breaker operating time and fault clearance time are also displayed in the GUI.

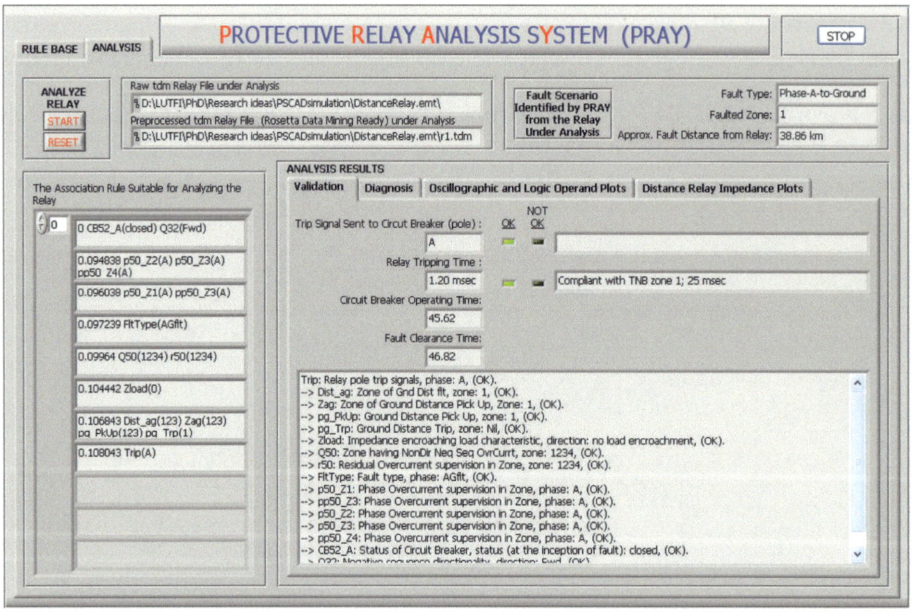

Figure 7. GUI for analysis of distance protective relay operations.

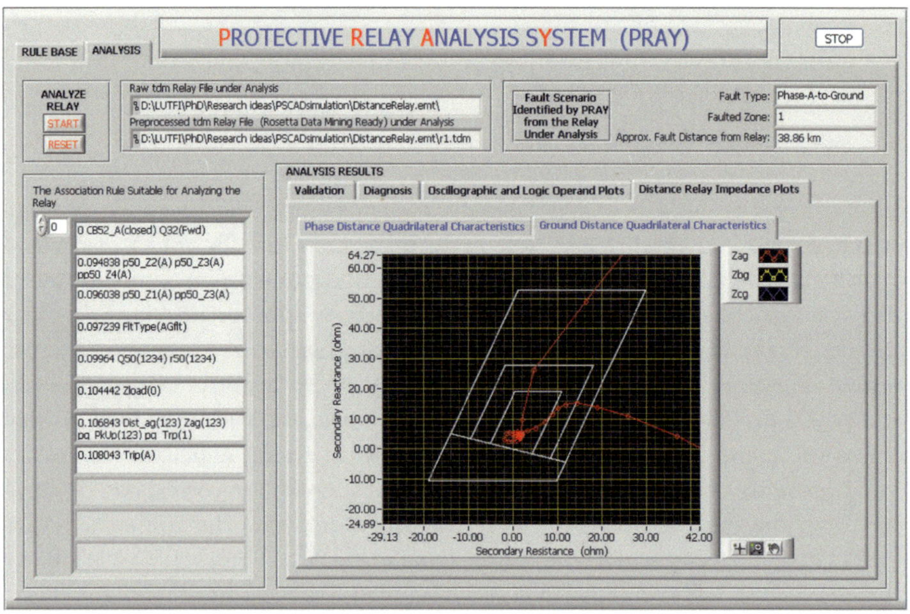

Figure 8. GUI for ground distance quadrilateral characteristics plots.

http://dx.doi.org/10.5772/63756

Figure 8 shows the graphical plots of ground impedance locus against respective ground distance quadrilateral characteristics. Since the fault is AG occurring in zone 1, it is noted that only trajectory of *Zag* traverses through into zone 1 of the ground quadrilateral characteristics and all phase impedances stay as outliers of the phase quadrilateral characteristics as expected.

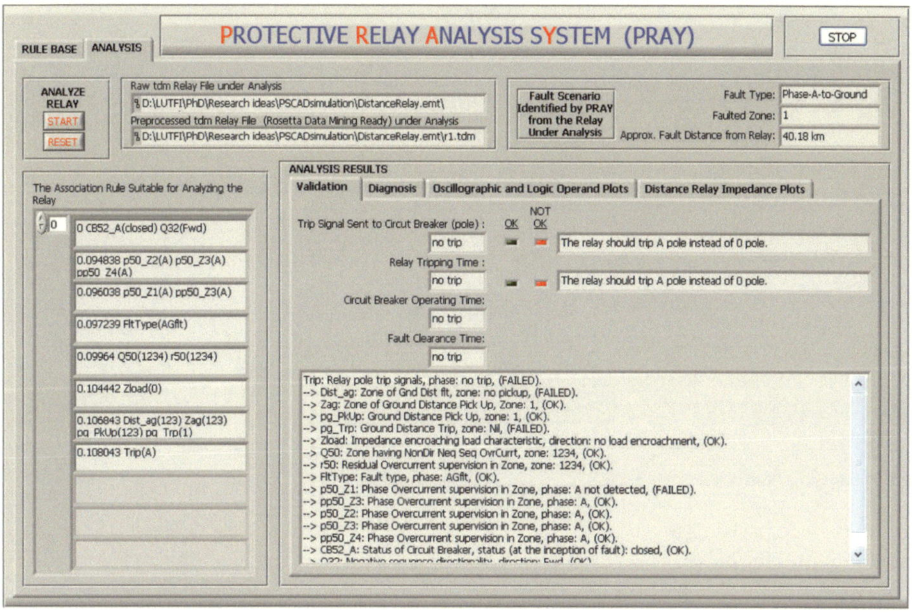

Figure 9. Validation of misoperative relay.

Figure 9 illustrates a screenshot of PRAY's validation for a distance relay that had failed to operate (maloperated) when the transmission line it was protecting was subjected to a zone-1-AG fault. PRAY discovered that an AG fault had occurred in one of the relays under analysis at approximately 40 km forward its location in the substation. (This is actually the same fault occurred in the above analysis of the same relay operating successfully.) From this information, an appropriate relay *CD*-association rule had been chosen as the hypothesis (similar to the above) and used to validate that appropriate measures had not been taken to clear the fault. The consequent "Trip" was validated to have not sent a pole-A trip signal to the circuit breaker. The descending sequence of antecedents indicated that although there were correct operations of negative sequence overcurrent (*Q50*) and residual overcurrent supervision (*r50*) elements, signifying the impending A–G imbalanced fault, the zone-1 overcurrent supervision element (*p50_Z1*) had failed to do likewise. This was believed to have attributed to the relay's failure to trip. Looking at the operation logic of different protective elements at different levels of sequence in the Diagnosis field's hierarchical tree, it is apparent that the failure by the overcurrent element *p50_Z1* is diagnosed to be the possible cause of the relay maloperation. Finding the symptom related to the malfunctional *p50_Z1* element as shown in **Figure 10** reveals that an incorrect threshold setting could have caused its failure.

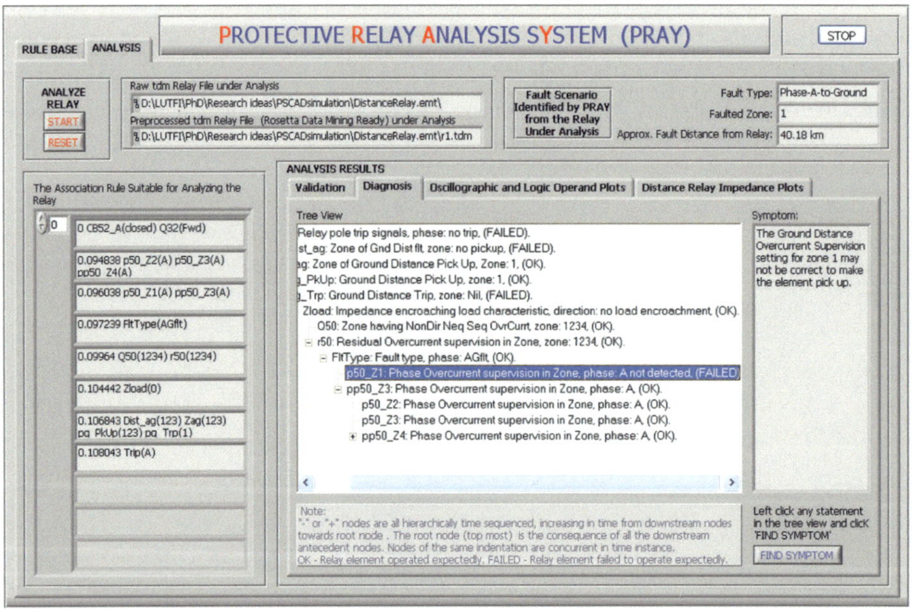

Figure 10. Diagnosis of misoperative relay.

5. Summary

The developed Protective Relay Analysis (PRAY) Expert System has demonstrated how the problems related to the maintenance of rule base of an Expert System can be addressed. By collating all the necessary relay *CD*-association rules discovered previously from the earlier KDD processes involving integrated-Rough-Set-and-Genetic-Algorithm data mining, Rule Quality Measure, and rule interestingness and importance judgments (as discussed in the authors' cited works), a maintainable knowledge base for inference strategy can be conveniently prepared. Although this study revolves around analyzing a modeled distance relay's big event data by hypothesis discovery, validation, and diagnosis, it is envisaged that using this approach a more rigorous analysis implementation of actual protective relay of different types can be embarked on.

Acknowledgements

This work was supported by the Universiti Putra Malaysia under the Geran Putra IPB scheme with the project no. GP-IPB/2013/9412101.

Nomenclature

http://dx.doi.org/10.5772/63756

C	rule condition attribute(s)
CB52_B	status of circuit breaker.
$C \Rightarrow D$	relay decision rule, general term for $(C \overset{assoc}{\Rightarrow} D)$ and $(C \overset{pred}{\Rightarrow} D)$
$(C \overset{assoc}{\Rightarrow} D)$	relay *CD*-association rule
$(C \overset{pred}{\Rightarrow} D)$	relay *CD*-prediction rule
CD-association rule	a relay association rule associating between *C* and *D*
CD-decision alg.	a set of relay prediction rules that predict *D* from *C* (alg. is algorithm)
CD-prediction rule	rule that predicts *D* from *C*
CNF	conjunctive normal form (i.e., product of sum (POS) in Boolean algebra).
COMTRADE	common format for transient data exchange, an IEEE file format
D	rule decision attribute
Dist_bg	zone of Gnd Dist flt (ground distance fault)
DNF	disjunctive normal form (i.e., sum of product (SOP) in Boolean algebra)
DS/DT	decision system/decision table
$f_C(D)$	discernibility function
FltType	fault type
GA	genetic algorithm
G2	*G2* Likelihood ratio statistic, a rule quality measure
IS	information system
KDD	Knowledge discovery in database
$M_C(D)$	*D*-discernibility matrix of *C*
p50_Z1	phase overcurrent supervision in zone
pg_PkUp	ground distance pick-up
pg_Trp	ground distance trip
PRAY	Protective relay analysis system, an Expert System
Q32	negative sequence directionality
Q50	zone having NonDir Neq Seq OvrCurrt (nondirectional negative sequence overcurrent)
r50	residual overcurrent supervision in zone
$RED_D(C)$	*D*-reducts of *C*, sets of reduced number of indispensable attributes
RST	Rough set theory
$M\ (f_C(D))$	multiset
$M\ (f_C(D))_{\text{Min Hit Set}}$	minimal hitting set
SOP	sum of products

Trip	relay pole trip signals
U∣*IND*(*D*)	indiscernibility-relation/equivalence-class/elementary-sets about universe of relay events *U* with respect to *D*
Zbg	zone of ground distance pick-up.
Zload	impedance encroaching load characteristic

Author details

Mohammad Lutfi Othman[1*], Ishak Aris[1] and Thammaiah Ananthapadmanabha[2]

*Address all correspondence to: lutfi@upm.edu.my

1 Center for Advanced Power and Energy Research, Department of Electrical and Electronics Engineering, Faculty of Engineering, Universiti Putra Malaysia, Serdang, Selangor, Malaysia

2 Department of Electrical and Electronics Engineering, The National Institute of Engineering, Mysore, Karnataka, India

References

[1] M. Ennas, L. Budler, T. W. Cease, A. Elneweihi, E. Guro, and M. Kezunovic. Potential applications of expert systems to power system protection. IEEE Transaction on Power Delivery. 1994;9(2):720–728.

[2] C. Fukui and J. Kawakami. An expert system fault section estimation using information from protective relays and circuit breakers. IEEE Transaction on Power Delivery. 1986;1(4):83–90.

[3] Y. Sun and C. C. Liu. RETEX (Relay Testing Expert): an expert system for analysis of relay testing data. IEEE Transaction on Power Delivery. 1992;7(2):986–994.

[4] D. Kosy, V. Grinberg, and M. Siegel. Screening digital relay data to detect power network fault response anomalies. In: SPIE Proc. 2nd International Symposium on Measurement Technology and Intelligent Instruments (ISMTII); Wuhan, People Republic of China; 29 Oct–5 Nov 1993.

[5] M. Kezunovic, P. Spasojevic, C. Fromen, and D. Sevcik. An expert system for transmission substation event analysis. IEEE Transaction on Power Delivery. 1993;8(4):1942–1949.

[6] M. Kezunovic, I. Rikalo, and C. W. Fromen. Expert system reasoning streamlines disturbance analysis. IEEE Computer Applications in Power. 1994;7(2):15–19.

[7] M. Kezunovic, I. Rikalo, C. W. Fromen, and D. R. Sevcik. New automated fault analysis approaches using intelligent system technologies. CiteSeerx Scientific Literature Digital Library and Search Engine, College of Info. Sci. and Tech., Pennsylvania State Univ [Internet]. 1998 [Updated: 1998]. Available from: http://eppe.tamu.edu/k/ee/china94.pdf [Accessed: 21 Dec 2015].

[8] M. Kezunovic and X. Luo. Automated analysis of protective relay data. In: CIRED 18th International Conference on Electricity Distribution; Turin; 2005.

[9] S. MacArthur, J. McDonald, S. Bell, and G. Burt. Expert systems and model based reasoning for protection performance analysis. In: IEE Colloquium on Artificial Intelligence Applications in Power Systems; 1995.

[10] X. Luo and M. Kezunovic. Fault analysis based on integration of digital relay and DFR data. In: IEEE Power Engineering Society General Meeting; 12–16 June 2005.

[11] Z. Wen-jing and J. Qing-quan. Research and simulation of an expert system on the wide-area back-up protection system. In: IET 9th International Conference on Developments in Power Systems Protection (DPSP 2008); Glasgow, UK; 17–20 March 2008.

[12] K. Tuitemwong and S. Premrudeepreechacharn. Expert system for protective devices coordination in radial distribution network with small power producers. In: IEEE Lausanne POWERTECH; Lausanne; 2007.

[13] K. Tuitemwong and S. Premrudeepreechacharn. Expert system for protection coordination of distribution system with distributed generators. International Journal of Electrical Power and Energy Systems. 2011;33(3):466–471.

[14] M. M. Saha, E. Rosolowski, and J. Izykowski. Artificial Intelligent Application to Power System Protection [Internet]. 2000. Available from: http://citeseer.ist.psu.edu/393733.html. [Accessed: 23 Dec 2015].

[15] M. L. Othman, I. Aris, S. M. Abdullah, M. L. Ali, and M. R. Othman. Knowledge discovery in distance relay event report: a comparative data-mining strategy of rough set theory with decision tree. IEEE Transaction on Power Delivery. 2010;25(4):2264–2287.

[16] M. L. Othman, I. Aris, M. R. Othman, and H. Osman. Rough-set-based timing characteristic analyses of distance protective relay. Applied Soft Computing. 2012;12(8):2053–2062.

[17] M. L. Othman, I. Aris, M. R. Othman, and H. Osman. Rough-set-and-genetic-algorithm based data mining and rule quality measure to hypothesize distance protective relay operation characteristics from relay event report. International Journal of Electrical Power and Energy Systems. 2011;33(8):1437–1456.

[18] M. L. Othman, I. Aris, and N. I. Abdul Wahab. Modeling and simulation of industrial numerical distance relay aimed at knowledge discovery in resident event report.

Simulation: Transactions of Society for Modelling and Simulation International. 2014;90(6):660–686.

[19] A. Øhrn. ROSETTA Technical Reference Manual. Trondheim, Norway: Norwegian University of Science and Technology; 2000.

[20] D. S. Hockbaum. Approximation Algorithms for NP-Hard Problems. Boston, MA: PWS Publishing Company; 1996.

[21] A. Øhrn. Discernibility and Rough Sets in Medicine: Tools and Applications. Trondheim, Norway: Norwegian University of Science and Technology; 1999.

[22] MAAC. Requirements for Protection System Operation Reporting and Analysis. Cleveland, Ohio: Mid Atlantic Area Council; 2003.

[23] N. Instruments. LabVIEW Basics I Introduction Course Manual. Austin, TX: National Instruments Corporation; 2006.

[24] A. Øhrn, J. Komorowski, A. Skowron, and P. Synak. The design and implementation of a knowledge discovery toolkit based on rough sets: The ROSETTA system. In: L. Polkowski and A. Skowron, editors. Rough Sets in Knowledge Discovery 1: Methodology and Applications, Studies in Fuzziness and Soft Computing. Heidelberg, Germany: Physica-Verlag, Springer; 1998. pp. 376–399.

[25] N. Instruments. DIAdem: Data Mining, Analysis, and Report Generation. Austin, TX: National Instrument Corporation; 2005.

Chapter 2

Real-World Treatment Patterns and Outcomes among Elderly Acute Myeloid Leukemia Patients in the United States

Sacha Satram- Hoang, Carolina Reyes,
Deborah Hurst, Khang Q. Hoang and
Bruno C. Medeiros

Additional information is available at the end of the chapter

http://dx.doi.org/10.5772/63758

Abstract

Over half of patients diagnosed with acute myeloid leukemia (AML) are 65 years or older. Using the linked SEER-Medicare database, we conducted a retrospective cohort analysis to examine patient characteristics, treatment patterns, and survival among the elderly AML patients in routine clinical practice. Out of 29,857 patients with AML in the database, 8336 were eligible for inclusion in the study. The inclusion criteria included a diagnosis with first primary AML between January 1, 2000 and December 31, 2009, >66 years of age, and continuous enrollment in Medicare Parts A and B in the year before diagnosis. Forty percent ($N = 3327$) of the cohort received chemotherapy within 3 months after diagnosis. The multivariable overall survival analyses showed a lower risk of death among those receiving intensive and hypomethylating agent therapies compared with no therapy. Among the younger cohort, a significant lower mortality was also noted with receipt of allogeneic hematopoietic stem cell transplantation. Over the past decade, about 60% of the elderly AML patients remain untreated in routine clinical practice. Use of antileukemic therapy was associated with a significant survival benefit and provides further support that age alone should not deter the use of guideline-recommended therapies particularly because of the high disparities in outcomes between treatment receipt and palliative care in this elderly cohort.

Keywords: acute myeloid leukemia, immunotherapy, chemotherapy, elderly patients, survival

1. Introduction

The American Cancer Society estimates that about 20,830 new cases of acute myeloid leukemia (AML) will be diagnosed in the United States in 2015 and 10,460 people will die of the disease [1]. Incidence of AML increases with age, with a median age at diagnosis of 66 years making it primarily a disease of the elderly [2]. Survival rates decline with age and AML is the leading cause of mortality from leukemia in the United States [3, 4].

The management of older adults with AML poses a difficult clinical challenge as they are more likely to have comorbidities and poorer performance status which can limit treatment options and tolerability. Treatment efficacy and tolerability have been shown to deteriorate markedly with age [5]. Although intensive combination chemotherapy is frequently chosen to achieve complete remission and long-term survival, fewer than half of elderly patients receive treatment and their outcomes remain dismal [5–7]. Conventional chemotherapy treatments are highly toxic and may increase early death rates in patients 65 and older and these patients are alternatively given low intensity treatment or palliation only [7, 8]. However, without treatment, patients succumb to their illness within weeks to months of diagnosis [9].

For medically fit older patients (>60 years), the National Comprehensive Cancer Network (NCCN) recommend treatment with a combination of an anthracycline and standard dose cytarabine while for medically unfit older adults with poor physical function or unfavorable risk disease, the NCCN recommends less intensive chemotherapy with DNA hypomethylating agents, low-dose cytarabine, or supportive care alone [10]. Allogeneic hematopoietic stem cell transplantation (HSCT) is rarely used in older patients due to significant comorbidities and higher risk of transplant-related morbidity and mortality [11, 12]. Even so, data from the Swedish Acute Leukemia Registry have demonstrated that the majority of patients <80 years are able to tolerate intensive treatment and have shown benefits in spite of deteriorating organ function [8, 13].

Elderly, Medicare aged patients constitute the majority of patients with cancer in the United States, but only 1–2% of them are enrolled in randomized clinical trials (RCTs) providing a limited evidence base in which to evaluate treatment efficacy and safety in this population [14–16]. Advanced age or the presence of significant comorbidity was the most frequently cited factors for clinical trial ineligibility [17]. The incidence of AML is expected to increase due to the aging population, and given the limited treatment options and clinical trial participation among the elderly, we examined Medicare beneficiaries diagnosed with AML from a large population-based cancer registry. The objectives of this analysis were to describe treatment patterns during the study time period, to examine factors predictive of receiving therapy, and to identify factors associated with prognosis among older AML patients in real-world clinical practice.

http://dx.doi.org/10.5772/63758

2. Methods

2.1. Data sources

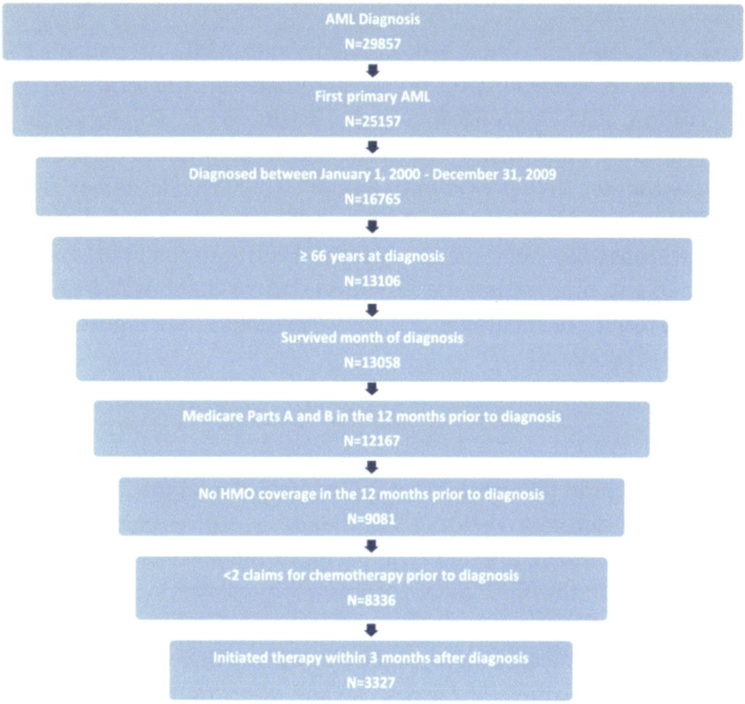

Figure 1. Schematic of inclusion/exclusion criteria.

This study utilized linked data from two large population-based data sources of Medicare beneficiaries with incident cancer identified in the Surveillance, Epidemiology, and End Results (SEER) program tumor registries. The database contains more than 3.3 million persons with cancer. Details of the linked SEER-Medicare database have been published elsewhere [18]. Briefly, the database combines clinical, demographic, cancer diagnosis, survival, and cause of death information with medical claims (hospital, physician, outpatient, home health, and hospice bills) for adults ≥65 diagnosed with cancer and enrolled in Medicare Part A (inpatient care, skilled nursing, home healthcare, and hospice care) and Part B (outpatient and physician services). The SEER is a nationally representative collection of 18 population-based registries of all incident cancers from diverse geographic areas covering approximately 26% of the US population. The registries monitor cancer trends, and provide continuous information on cancer incidence, extent of disease at diagnosis, therapy, and patient survival. A 98% case ascertainment is mandated with annual quality-assurance studies. The majority of persons aged 65 years and older in the SEER are successfully matched to their Medicare enrollment files [18]. All Medicare beneficiaries receive Part A coverage and approximately 95% of beneficiaries subscribe to Part B. The SEER-Medicare linkage used in this study included all

Medicare eligible cancer patients appearing in the SEER data through 2009 and their Medicare claims for Part A and Part B through 2010. Institutional review board approval was waived because the SEER-Medicare data lack personal identifiers.

2.2. Study cohort

The SEER-Medicare dataset contained 29,857 patients with AML. All patients had microscopically confirmed AML diagnosis based on the International Classification of Diseases for Oncology (3rd edition, ICD-O-3) histology codes in the SEER. For inclusion in the study, patients were restricted to those with a first primary AML in order to exclude therapy-related AML, diagnosed within the time period from January 1, 2000 to December 31, 2009, ≥66 years of age, and enrolled in Medicare Parts A and B for a full 12 months before diagnosis date. Study exclusion criteria were as follows: (1) diagnosis at death, (2) enrollment in a health maintenance organization (HMO) any time within the 12 months before diagnosis since HMO claims are unavailable, and (3) receipt of chemotherapy before diagnosis. See **Figure 1** for the schematic of inclusion/exclusion process.

2.3. Study variables

Key study measures include patient demographics (age, race/ethnicity, gender, income, and education level); clinical characteristics (AML diagnosis, tumor characteristics, risk status, comorbidity burden, treatment, and survival time). In the absence of cytogenetic data and molecular abnormalities in the SEER data, prior myelodysplastic syndrome (MDS) or myeloproliferative neoplasm (MPN) was used as a proxy for high-risk patients and was identified using diagnosis codes in Medicare Parts A and B claim files. MDS or MPN that transforms into AML are poor prognostic features of the disease and occur more commonly among elderly patients [19]. Performance status, such as Eastern Cooperative Oncology Group (ECOG), is not available in the dataset so Medicare claims were used to identify poor performance indicators (PPI) which include oxygen and related respiratory supplies, wheelchair and supplies, home health agency services, and skilled nursing facility services occurring in the 12 months before diagnosis [20]. The National Cancer Institute (NCI) comorbidity index [21] is the gold standard in SEER-Medicare to capture comorbidity burden using diagnosis and procedure codes to identify the 15 noncancer comorbidities from the Charlson Comorbidity Index [22] that occurred in the 12 months before cancer diagnosis.

In the Medicare claims files, International Classification of Disease (9th revision) Clinical Modification (ICD-9-CM) procedure codes were used to identify chemotherapy administration while the Healthcare Common Procedural Coding System (HCPCS) "J" codes were used to identify the specific intravenous chemotherapy administered [23]. The first claim for chemotherapy had to appear within 3 months of the AML diagnosis date, and patients were classified into one of three treatment groups using all chemotherapies received during the first 60 days after date of chemotherapy initiation. Those receiving low intensity therapy with a DNA methyltransferase (DNMT) inhibitor such as Azacitidine or Decitabine were classified into the hypomethylating agents or "HMA Therapy" group; and those receiving aggressive induction therapy with Cytarabine + Anthracycline were classified into the "Intensive

Therapy" group. Given that chemotherapy for AML is usually administered during inpatient stays, specific chemotherapy agent identification using J codes was not possible in about 70% of treated patients because inpatient stays are paid according to ICD-9 diagnosis or procedures codes only. Allogeneic HSCT was also identified using ICD-9-CM and HCPCS codes in the patient's Medicare claim files that occurred in the study follow-up period.

2.4. Outcome measures

The primary endpoint was overall survival after the AML diagnosis. Overall survival was measured from date of diagnosis to date of death. To assess the risk of early death (30-day mortality and 60-day mortality) after diagnosis, the "treated" group was limited to patients who received treatment within 30 days after diagnosis to minimize the introduction of immortal time bias into the analysis (period of follow-up time during which death cannot occur) [24]. All patients who were still alive at the end of the follow-up period (December 31, 2010) were censored.

2.5. Statistical analysis

Patient characteristics were compared with treatment status and treatment type using the Chi-square test for categorical variables and ANOVA or *t* test for continuous variables. We considered a p-value <0.05 to be statistically significant. Multivariate logistic regression was used to assess factors associated with receipt of treatment.

In the survival analyses, we made comparisons between the treated and Not Treated patients; between treated patients receiving HSCT and those who did not; and between HMA Therapy, Intensive Therapy, and No Treatment groups. The Kaplan-Meier survival analysis was used to plot survival curves. A time-varying Cox regression model with treatment as a time-dependent factor was used to account for variation in treatment initiation between groups. Other independent variables included in the Cox model were selected demographic and clinical characteristics. All statistical analyses were performed using SAS software, version 9.1.3 (SAS Institute Inc., Cary, NC, USA).

3. Results

3.1. Treatment patterns

Treatment rates increased over the study time period from 35% in 2000 to 50% in 2009 (**Figure 2**). Of the 8336 patients who met all study criteria, 3327 (40%) received treatment with chemotherapy within 3 months of diagnosis and 5009 (60%) did not. As age and comorbidity burden increased, likelihood of treatment was found to decrease (**Figures 3** and **4**).

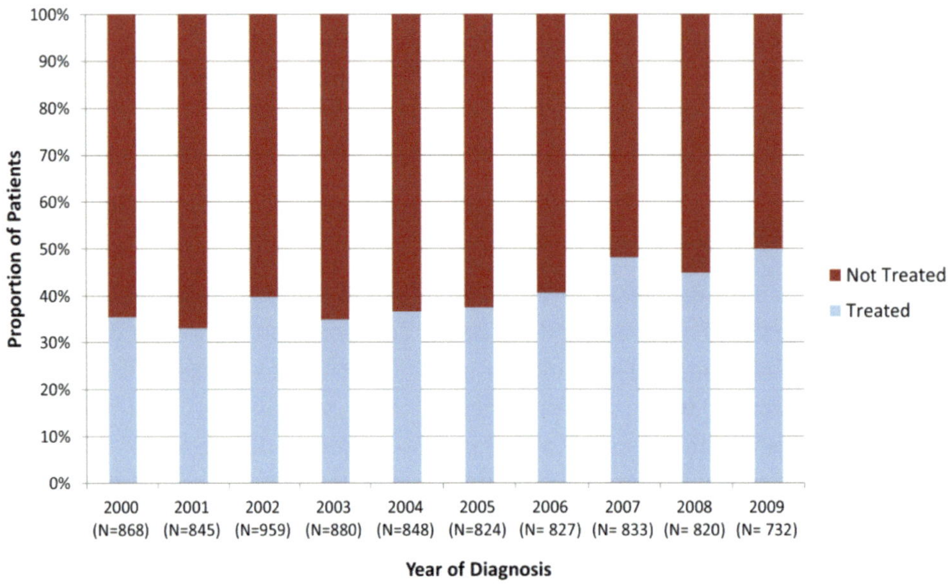

Figure 2. Treatment status by year of diagnosis.

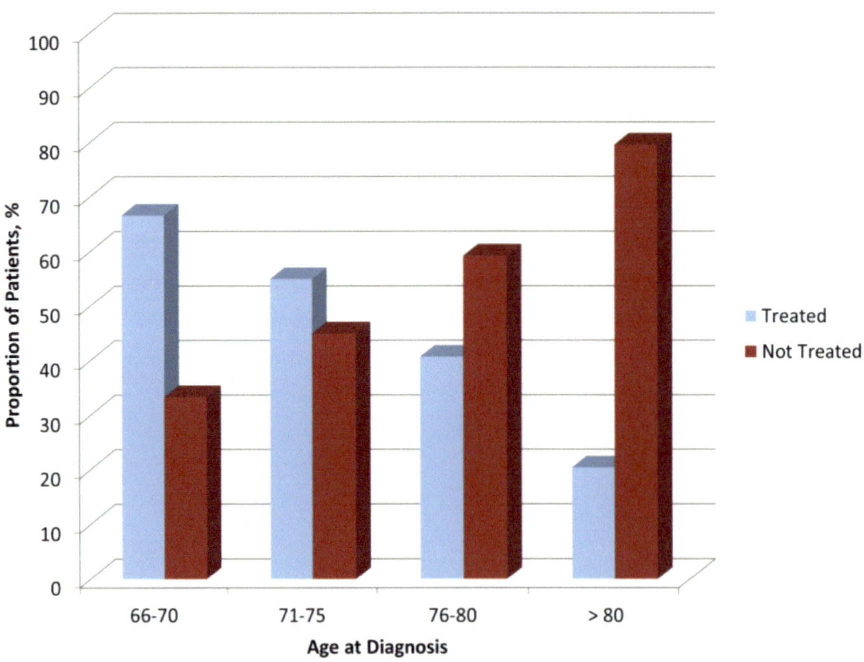

Figure 3. Treatment status by age.

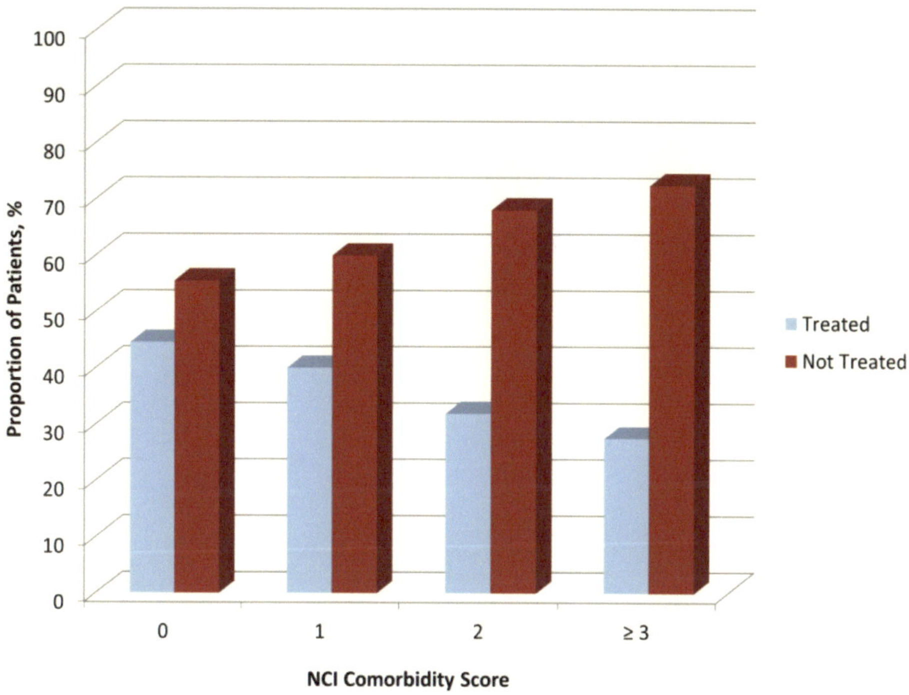

Figure 4. Treatment status by comorbidity burden.

3.2. Cohort characteristics and the odds of treatment receipt

Table 1 shows the baseline patient characteristics of the cohort. Overall, the majority of patients were over 75 years of age (63%), male, white, and married. In the logistic regression model of factors associated with the odds of not receiving treatment with chemotherapy or HSCT, increasing age and increasing comorbidity score were confirmed to significantly decrease the likelihood of receiving treatment. Patients of black or African ancestry were 30% less likely to receive treatment than white patients. Being widowed, separated/divorced, having a history of MDS or presence of PPI significantly decreased the likelihood of receiving treatment.

Table 2 shows the baseline patient characteristics by the type of treatment received. Compared with other treatment groups, patients receiving Intensive Therapy were younger, more likely male, married, less secondary AML (prior MDS), less likely to have PPIs, and had lower comorbidity score. Similarities in age, comorbidity burden, and proportion with high-risk disease were noted in HMA Therapy and Not Treated patients.

Among treated patients, there were 276 (8%) who underwent HSCT therapy and 3051 (92%) who did not (**Table 2**). The HSCT patients were younger at diagnosis with a mean age of 73 compared with the non-HSCT group (75 years; $p < 0.0001$) and were more likely to be male.

Characteristic	**Total (N = 8336)**		**Odds of no treatment**		
	n	%	**OR**[a]	**95% CI**	***p*-value**
Age at diagnosis					
66–70	1322	15.9	ref		
71–75	1774	21.3	1.64	1.41–1.91	<0.0001
76–80	1971	23.6	2.86	2.46–3.32	<0.0001
>80	3269	39.2	7.40	6.36–8.61	<0.0001
Sex					
Male	4331	52.0	ref		
Female	4005	48.0	0.97	0.87–1.07	0.5193
Race/ethnicity					
White	7285	87.4	ref		
Black	502	6.0	1.30	1.04–1.62	0.0045
Other/unknown	549	6.6	0.87	0.71–1.05	0.4119
Marital status					
Married	4373	52.5	ref		
Widowed	2492	29.9	1.29	1.13–1.46	0.0036
Separated/divorced	543	6.5	1.34	1.10–1.64	0.0128
Single	535	6.4	1.21	0.99–1.48	0.0796
Unknown	393	4.7	1.31	1.04–1.66	0.0359
Prior MDS					
No	6896	82.7	ref		
Yes	1440	17.3	1.18	1.03–1.34	0.0151
PPI					
No	7280	87.3	ref		
Yes	1056	12.7	2.02	1.69–2.41	<0.0001
NCI comorbidity score					
0	4266	51.2	ref		
1	2104	25.2	1.07	0.95–1.21	0.1017
2	1018	12.2	1.41	1.20–1.66	0.0326
≥3	948	11.4	1.56	1.31–1.86	0.0004

[a]*Model also includes geographic region, income,and year of diagnosis.*

Table 1. Factors associated with the odds of NOT receiving chemotherapy or HSCT.

http://dx.doi.org/10.5772/63758

Characteristic	**Not Treated (*N* = 5009)**	**HMA Therapy (*N* = 345)**	**Intensive Therapy (*N* = 124)**	***p***	**HSCT (*N* = 276)**	**No HSCT (*N* = 3051)**	***p***
	(%)	**(%)**	**(%)**	**(%)**	**(%)**	**(%)**	
Age at diagnosis							
66–70	8.8	13.6	39.5	<0.0001	44.6	24.8	<0.0001
71–75	15.9	24.1	31.5		25.4	29.7	
76–80	23.3	25.5	16.1		14.5	25.0	
>80	51.9	36.8	12.9		15.6	20.5	
Sex							
Male	49.9	59.1	62.1	0.0002	61.6	54.5	0.0228
Female	50.1	40.9	37.9		38.4	45.5	
Race/ethnicity							
White	87.2	90.4	87.9	0.2092	88.4	87.6	0.7118
Nonwhite	6.7	9.6	12.1		11.6	12.4	
Marital status							
Married	46.8	61.2	71.0	<0.0001	59.4	61.1	0.0851
Widowed	35.3	21.4	15.3		18.5	22.1	
Separated/divorced	6.5	5.5	13.6[a]		10.1	6.2	
Single	6.4	6.7			7.6	6.4	
Unknown	5.1	5.2			4.3	4.2	
Prior MDS							
No	81.0	79.1	100[a]	0.0026	88.8	85.0	0.0920
Yes	19.0	20.9			11.2	15.0	
PPI							
No	83.2	91.3	100[a]	<0.0001	94.2	93.4	0.6245
Yes	16.8	8.7				5.8	6.6
NCI comorbidity score							
0	47.3	50.7	55.6	0.1113	55.8	57.2	0.2711
1	25.2	25.8	25.8		22.8	25.5	
2	13.8	11.6	18.5[a]		10.9	9.7	
≥3	13.7	11.9				10.5	7.6

[a]Cells with counts of less than 11 are combined in compliance with the National Cancer Institute data in agreement with small cell sizes.

Table 2. Baseline patient characteristics by type of treatment received.

3.3. Overall survival by chemotherapy type

Covariates	N	Total[a] (N = 5478)		≤75 years[a] (N = 1457)		>75 years[a] (N = 4021)	
Treatment		**HR**	**95% CI**	**HR**	**95% CI**	**HR**	**95% CI**
Not treated (ref)	5009						
HMA therapy	345	0.52	0.47–0.59	0.54	0.45–0.66	0.50	0.44–0.58
Intensive therapy	124	0.33	0.27–0.41	0.30	0.23–0.39	0.38	0.26–0.54
Age at diagnosis							
66–70 (ref)	537						
71–75	920	1.31	1.17–1.46				
76–80	1276	1.42	1.27–1.58				
>80	2745	1.68	1.52–1.86				
Sex							
Male (ref)	2780						
Female	2698	1.01	0.96–1.08	0.99	0.88–1.11	1.03	0.96–1.10
Race/ethnicity							
White (ref)	4788						
Black	350	0.96	0.86–1.07	1.04	0.85–1.28	0.92	0.80–1.05
Other/unknown	340	0.89	0.79–1.00	0.93	0.74–1.16	0.86	0.75–0.98
Marital status							
Married (ref)	2644						
Widowed	1859	1.12	1.05–1.20	1.33	1.14–1.56	1.10	1.02–1.19
Separated/divorced	349	1.11	0.99–1.25	1.09	0.89–1.33	1.07	0.93–1.23
Single	349	1.18	1.05–1.32	1.31	1.07–1.59	1.12	0.97–1.28
Unknown	277	1.00	0.88–1.13	0.94	0.73–1.20	1.01	0.87–1.18
Prior MDS							
No (ref)	4445						
Yes	1033	0.97	0.91–1.04	1.03	0.89–1.19	0.95	0.88–1.03
PPI							
No (ref)	4605						
Yes	873	1.30	1.20–1.40	1.58	1.32–1.90	1.26	1.16–1.38
NCI comorbidity score							
0 (ref)	2611						
1	1383	1.18	1.10–1.26	1.35	1.18–1.54	1.12	1.03–1.21

Covariates	N	Total[a] (N = 5478)		≤75 years[a] (N = 1457)		>75 years[a] (N = 4021)	
Treatment		HR	95% CI	HR	95% CI	HR	95% CI
2	749	1.29	1.19–1.41	1.43	1.20–1.70	1.25	1.14–1.38
≥3	735	1.38	1.26–1.51	1.40	1.16–1.69	1.35	1.21–1.49

[a]Model also includes geographic region, income, and year of diagnosis.

Table 3. Adjusted overall survival by treatment type.

Patients receiving Intensive Therapy had longer unadjusted median overall survival (18.9 months) compared with patients receiving HMA Therapy (6.6 months) and those Not Treated (1.5 months; log rank p <0.0001). In the multivariable survival analysis (**Table 3**), significantly lower risks of death were noted among patients treated with Intensive Therapy and HMA Therapy compared with Not Treated with similar mortality risk reductions maintained in the younger (≤75) and older (>75) cohorts. Other factors found to be predictive of mortality include increasing age, increasing comorbidity score, and presence of PPIs.

3.4. Overall survival by HSCT

The unadjusted median overall survival was significantly higher for the HSCT (9.7 months) compared with the non-HSCT group (4.7 months; log rank p < 0.0001) and this survival benefit was supported in the multivariable survival analysis (**Table 4**), where a statistically significant, 21% lower risk of death in the HSCT group was found compared with the non-HSCT group. Stratifying by age, the lower risk of death among the HSCT group was only supported in the younger cohort (≤75 years old).

Treatment	Treated[a](N = 3321)			≤75 years[a] (N = 1854)			>75 years[a] (N = 1467)		
	HR	95% CI	p	HR	95% CI	p	HR	95% CI	p
No HSCT (ref)									
HSCT	0.80	0.70–0.92	0.0015	0.63	0.53–0.75	<0.0001	1.21	0.96–1.53	0.1041

[a]Adjusted for age, sex, race, marital status, geographic region, income, year of diagnosis, prior MDS, PPI, and NCI comorbidity index.

Table 4. Adjusted overall survival among treated patients with and without HSCT.

4. Discussion

Treatment for elderly patients diagnosed with AML has increased over time from the 34% reported by Lang et al. between 1991 and 2001 [7] to the 40% reported in our study between 2000 and 2010. However, the 60% of elderly AML patients who remain untreated following diagnosis represents a large unmet need in this patient population. We observed a significant survival benefit with receiving antileukemic therapy even among the HMA Therapy group who had similar characteristics to the untreated group. Our multivariate analysis demonstrated a greater reduction in mortality among patients receiving Intensive Therapy compared with HMA Therapy, but both therapeutic options appeared to be equally better than supportive measures when the cohorts were properly matched for relevant confounders. Results from prior RCTs also support our findings and have demonstrated not only an improvement in complete remission rate, but also an improvement in overall survival for AML patients aged 65 years or older treated with intensive chemotherapy [25] and HMA Therapy [26] compared with supportive measures only.

The current results also draw attention to the perception that elderly AML is an untreatable disease and conventional chemotherapy is usually withheld due to toxicity and high early death rates. Our results, however, confirm findings from other registry-based analyses that showed elderly AML patients who received treatment exhibited a lower early death rate compared with untreated patients or palliation after adjustment for confounding factors [8, 13, 27]. Despite the overall improvement in early death rates in the treated versus untreated groups, subsets of patients older than 80 years or those with poor performance or higher comorbidity burden did experience higher risks of early death suggesting caution in use of therapy within these subgroups.

The HSCT therapy was associated with a significant lower risk of death compared with patients receiving chemotherapy only and the survival benefit was even more pronounced in the younger cohort (≤75 years) with no benefit in the >75 years old subset. Although our observations are at best hypothesis generating, they raise the question of whether allogeneic HSCT provides therapeutic benefit to AML patients older than 75 years of age. Although use of myeloablative allogeneic HSCT is rare among older unfit patients, reduced-intensity conditioning (RIC) of the allogeneic HSCT has shown encouraging results in the postremission setting [11, 12, 28] and is considered an additional treatment option after complete response from induction therapy among older patients ≥60 years [10]. In fact, a recent uncontrolled study demonstrated that reduced-intensity conditioning HSCT as postremission therapy was well tolerated in selected older patients with AML, and survival compared favorably to historical patients treated without HSCT [29]. However, in the "real world," chronologic age remains a driving factor in receiving HSCT as only 8% of patients in the current study who received chemotherapy underwent subsequent HSCT therapy. The randomized clinical trials are needed to define the role of allogeneic HSCT as postremission therapy in this cohort of patients.

The results show that patients receiving Intensive Therapy were younger, had less secondary AML, were less likely to have indicators of poor performance, and had lower comorbidity burden compared with patients receiving HMA Therapy and No Treatment, and this may be related to physician beliefs that elderly patients are less able to tolerate more aggressive treatments [5, 30–32]. Undertreatment because of age, independent of comorbidities, occurs in other oncology studies, and may be due to patient preferences, physicians' tendencies to treat patients according to their chronologic age, and a lack of evidence-based guidelines for treating older patients [33, 34]. In two prior RCTs where preselection of conventional care regimens was performed before subjects were randomized, those assigned to aggressive therapies had a median of 5–8 years younger than their counterparts assigned to less intensive regimens [35, 36]. These age disparities in treatment patterns are associated with higher mortality in older AML patients [5, 6] and our results provide further support that demographic factors such as age should not discourage the use of guideline-recommended therapies.

Treatment receipt also varied by gender, socioeconomic factors, geographic region, and marital status, similar to patterns observed in prior oncology research [37–39]. Even after adjustment for known confounders, married patients were more likely to receive treatment and had better outcomes compared with unmarried patients [39] and may indicate that marital status is a surrogate of social-economic support in this patient population. Reducing the disparity of nonclinical factors such as income and geographic region on receipt of cancer therapy may reduce the adverse impact on outcomes among these patients. Further research is warranted to better quantify how nonclinical factors contribute to receipt of cancer therapy and outcomes.

4.1. Strengths and limitations

This unique dataset allowed us to examine all AML patients, both treated and untreated, and provided insight into treatment decisions and effectiveness of therapies in routine oncology practice among this underrepresented elderly patient population. Our analysis has several strengths including the large sample size from a population-based cancer registry, the diverse geographic representation of AML patients in the United States, and comprehensive, longitudinal data with medical claims from the time a person is eligible for Medicare until death regardless of residence or service area.

However, there are some limitations to the analysis that deserve mention. The SEER registry does not collect baseline molecular and cytogenetic information or performance status, and these factors influence clinicians' decisions to treat or the specific regimen to administer. Our proxies for stage (including claims for prior MDS as a marker of disease severity) and performance status (including claims to identify indicators of poor performance) may not adequately assess stage or performance status in all patients and may be subject to bias.

The results of the comparative effectiveness analysis should be interpreted with caution due to the large amount of missing data and resulting small sample size of treatment groups. Conventional chemotherapy treatments for AML are highly toxic [9] and generally require inpatient treatment. Inpatient stays are paid based on ICD-9 diagnosis or procedures codes only and not the specific chemotherapy J code administered. Therefore, we were unable to define the type of chemotherapy received for 70% of the treated cohort without the specific J code. Given that induction chemotherapy with curative intent in the outpatient setting is applied to very select elderly AML patients, our findings may not be representative of the general patient population receiving intensive induction therapy.

Finally, this analysis does not contain information regarding treatment patterns and outcomes of patients enrolled in HMO plans as these claims are not submitted to Medicare. Prior solid tumor studies found that HMO enrollees were diagnosed earlier and had better overall survival compared with fee-for-service (FFS) plan members [40, 41]. An investigation of how patient characteristics, treatment patterns, and prognosis may differ between these alternative healthcare plans and Medicare enrollees would be a productive area for additional evaluation.

In conclusion, our findings provide an important context for therapeutic selection that occurs in older patients with AML and suggests that age alone should not discourage the use of guideline-recommended therapies particularly because of the high disparities in outcomes between treatment receipt and palliative care. But even with treatment, outcomes remain dismal, and given this important unmet medical need, many new agents are currently in development for older patients with AML [42–45]. Moving forward, it will be important to identify patients less likely to be treated at diagnosis and design clinical trials to address the therapeutic challenges that exist in this cohort of patients.

Acknowledgements

Funding for this study was provided by Genentech, Inc. The authors would like to acknowledge Faiyaz Momin, MS, for programming support and Dr. Michelle Byrtek for her invaluable input on the statistical analyses. This study used the linked SEER-Medicare database. We acknowledge the efforts of the Applied Research Program, NCI (Bethesda, MD), the Office of Information Services, and the Office of Strategic Planning, Health Care Financing Administration (Baltimore, MD), Information Management Services, Inc. (Silver Spring, MD), and the Surveillance, Epidemiology, and End Results (SEER) Program tumor registries in the creation of the SEER-Medicare database. The interpretation and reporting of these data are the sole responsibility of the authors.

Author details

Sacha Satram- Hoang[1*], Carolina Reyes[2,3], Deborah Hurst[2], Khang Q. Hoang[1] and Bruno C. Medeiros[4]

*Address all correspondence to: sacha@qdresearch.com

1 Q.D. Research, Inc.,, Granite Bay, CA, USA

2 Genentech, Inc.,, South San Francisco, CA, USA

3 University of California San Francisco,, San Francisco, CA, USA

4 Stanford University, Stanford,, CA, USA

http://dx.doi.org/10.5772/63758

References

[1] American Cancer Society. *Cancer Facts & Figures 2015*. 2015 [cited 2015 December 9]; Available from: http://www.cancer.org/research/cancerfactsstatistics/cancerfactsfigures2015/.

[2] National Cancer Institute. *SEER Stat Fact Sheets: Acute Myeloid Leukemia*. Bethesda, MD. 2012 [November 2013]; Available from: http://seer.cancer.gov/statfacts/html/amyl.html.

[3] Yamamoto, J.F. and M.T. Goodman, *Patterns of leukemia incidence in the United States by subtype and demograp hic characteristics, 1997–2002*. Cancer Causes Control, 2008. 19(4): pp. 379–90.

[4] Siegel, R., D. Naishadham, and A. Jemal, *Cancer statistics, 2013*. CA Cancer J Clin, 2013. 63(1): pp. 11–30.

[5] Appelbaum, F.R., et al., *Age and acute myeloid leukemia*. Blood, 2006. 107(9): pp. 3481–5.

[6] Kantarjian, H., et al., *Results of intensive chemotherapy in 998 patients age 65 years or older with acute myeloid leukemia or high-risk myelodysplastic syndrome: predictive prognostic models for outcome*. Cancer, 2006. 106(5): pp. 1090–8.

[7] Lang, K., et al., *Trends in the treatment of acute myeloid leukaemia in the elderly*. Drugs Aging, 2005. 22(11): pp. 943–55.

[8] Juliusson, G., *Older patients with acute myeloid leukemia benefit from intensive chemotherapy: an update from the Swedish Acute Leukemia Registry*. Clin Lymphoma Myeloma Leuk, 2011. 11(Suppl 1): pp. S54–9.

[9] Williams, J.P. and H.L. Handler, *Antibody-targeted chemotherapy for the treatment of relapsed acute myeloid leukemia*. Am J Manag Care, 2000. 6(18 Suppl): pp. S975–85.

[10] National Comprehensive Cancer Network, *NCCN Clinical Practice Guidelines in Oncology: Acute Myeloid Leukemia Version 2.2014*. 2014 [August 30, 2014]; Available from: http://www.nccn.org/professionals/physician_gls/PDF/aml.pdf.

[11] Herr, A.L., et al., *HLA-identical sibling allogeneic peripheral blood stem cell transplantation with reduced intensity conditioning compared to autologous peripheral blood stem cell transplantation for elderly patients with de novo acute myeloid leukemia*. Leukemia, 2007. 21(1): pp. 129–35.

[12] Storb, R., *Can reduced-intensity allogeneic transplantation cure older adults with AML?* Best Pract Res Clin Haematol, 2007. 20(1): pp. 85–90.

[13] Juliusson, G., et al., *Age and acute myeloid leukemia: real world data on decision to treat and outcomes from the Swedish Acute Leukemia Registry*. Blood, 2009. 113(18): pp. 4179–87.

[14] Murthy, V.H., H.M. Krumholz, and C.P. Gross, *Participation in cancer clinical trials: race-, sex-, and age-based disparities*. JAMA, 2004. 291(22): pp. 2720–6.

[15] Hutchins, L.F., et al., *Underrepresentation of patients 65 years of age or older in cancer-treatment trials*. N Engl J Med, 1999. 341(27): pp. 2061–7.

[16] Gross, C.P., et al., *Cancer trial enrollment after state-mandated reimbursement*. J Natl Cancer Inst, 2004. 96(14): pp. 1063–9.

[17] Mengis, C., et al., *Assessment of differences in patient populations selected for excluded from participation in clinical phase III acute myelogenous leukemia trials*. J Clin Oncol, 2003. 21(21): pp. 3933–9.

[18] Warren, J.L., et al., *Overview of the SEER-Medicare data: content, research applications, and generalizability to the United States elderly population*. Med Care, 2002. 40(8 Suppl): p. IV-3-18.

[19] Vardiman, J.W., et al., *The 2008 revision of the World Health Organization (WHO) classification of myeloid neoplasms and acute leukemia: rationale and important changes*. Blood, 2009. 114(5): pp. 937–51.

[20] Davidoff, A.J., et al., *Chemotherapy and survival benefit in elderly patients with advanced non-small-cell lung cancer*. J Clin Oncol, 2010. 28(13): pp. 2191–7.

[21] Klabunde, C.N., et al., *A refined comorbidity measurement algorithm for claims-based studies of breast, prostate, colorectal, and lung cancer patients*. Ann Epidemiol, 2007. 17(8): pp. 584–90.

[22] Charlson, M.E., et al., *A new method of classifying prognostic comorbidity in longitudinal studies: development and validation*. J Chronic Dis, 1987. 40(5): pp. 373–83.

[23] Warren, J.L., et al., *Utility of the SEER-Medicare data to identify chemotherapy use*. Med Care, 2002. 40(8 Suppl): p. IV-55-61.

[24] Suissa, S., *Immortal time bias in pharmaco-epidemiology*. Am J Epidemiol, 2008. 167(4): pp. 492–9.

[25] Lowenberg, B., et al., *On the value of intensive remission-induction chemotherapy in elderly patients of 65+ years with acute myeloid leukemia: a randomized phase III study of the European Organization for Research and Treatment of Cancer Leukemia Group*. J Clin Oncol, 1989. 7(9): pp. 1268–74.

[26] Kantarjian, H.M., et al., *Multicenter, randomized, open-label, phase III trial of decitabine versus patient choice, with physician advice, of either supportive care or low-dose cytarabine for the treatment of older patients with newly diagnosed acute myeloid leukemia*. J Clin Oncol, 2012. 30(21): pp. 2670–7.

[27] Oran, B. and D.J. Weisdorf, *Survival for older patients with acute myeloid leukemia: a population-based study*. Haematologica, 2012. 97(12): pp. 1916–24.

[28] Estey, E., et al., *Prospective feasibility analysis of reduced-intensity conditioning (RIC) regimens for hematopoietic stem cell transplantation (HSCT) in elderly patients with acute myeloid leukemia (AML) and high-risk myelodysplastic syndrome (MDS).* Blood, 2007. 109(4): pp. 1395–400.

[29] Devine, S.M., et al., *Phase II study of allogeneic transplantation for older patients with acute myeloid leukemia in first complete remission using a reduced-intensity conditioning regimen: results from cancer and leukemia Group B 100103 (alliance for clinical trials in oncology)/blood and marrow transplant clinical trial network 0502.* J Clin Oncol, 2015. 33(35): pp. 4167–75.

[30] Juliusson, G., et al., *Attitude towards remission induction for elderly patients with acute myeloid leukemia influences survival.* Leukemia, 2006. 20(1): pp. 42–7.

[31] Buchner, T., et al., *Acute myeloid leukemia: treatment over 60.* Rev Clin Exp Hematol, 2002. 6(1): pp. 46–59; discussion 86–7.

[32] Nabhan, C., et al., *Analysis of very elderly (>/=80 years) non-hodgkin lymphoma: impact of functional status and co-morbidities on outcome.* Br J Haematol, 2012. 156(2): pp. 196–204.

[33] Dale, D.C., *Poor prognosis in elderly patients with cancer: the role of bias and undertreatment.* J Support Oncol, 2003. 1(4 Suppl 2): pp. 11–7.

[34] Oxnard, G.R., et al., *Non-small cell lung cancer in octogenarians: treatment practices and preferences.* J Thorac Oncol, 2007. 2(11): pp. 1029–35.

[35] Fenaux, P., et al., *Azacitidine prolongs overall survival compared with conventional care regimens in elderly patients with low bone marrow blast count acute myeloid leukemia.* J Clin Oncol, 2010. 28(4): pp. 562–9.

[36] Dombret, H., et al. *Results of a Phase 3, multicenter, randomized, open-label study of Azacitidine (AZA) vs conventional care regimens (CCR) in older patients with newly diagnosed acute myeloid leukemia (AML).* In: *19th Congress of the European Hematology Association* 2014. Milan, Italy.

[37] Wang, M., et al., *Ethnic variations in diagnosis, treatment, socioeconomic status, and survival in a large population-based cohort of elderly patients with non-Hodgkin lymphoma.* Cancer, 2008. 113(11): pp. 3231–41.

[38] Shavers, V.L. and M.L. Brown, *Racial and ethnic disparities in the receipt of cancer treatment.* J Natl Cancer Inst, 2002. 94(5): pp. 334–57.

[39] Aizer, A.A., et al., *Marital status and survival in patients with cancer.* J Clin Oncol, 2013. 31(31): pp. 3869–76.

[40] Kirsner, R.S., et al., *The effect of medicare health care delivery systems on survival for patients with breast and colorectal cancer.* Cancer Epidemiol Biomarkers Prev, 2006. 15(4): pp. 769–73.

[41] Merrill, R.M., et al., *Survival and treatment for colorectal cancer Medicare patients in two group/staff health maintenance organizations and the fee-for-service setting*. Med Care Res Rev, 1999. 56(2): pp. 177–96.

[42] Dohner, H., et al., *Randomized, phase 2 trial of low-dose cytarabine with or without volasertib in AML patients not suitable for induction therapy*. Blood, 2014. 124(9): pp. 1426–33.

[43] Lancet, J.E., et al., *Phase 2 trial of CPX-351, a fixed 5:1 molar ratio of cytarabine/daunorubicin, vs cytarabine/daunorubicin in older adults with untreated AML*. Blood, 2014. 123(21): pp. 3239–46.

[44] Burnett, A.K., et al., *Addition of gemtuzumab ozogamicin to induction chemotherapy improves survival in older patients with acute myeloid leukemia*. J Clin Oncol, 2012. 30(32): pp. 3924–31.

[45] Castaigne, S., et al., *Effect of gemtuzumab ozogamicin on survival of adult patients with de-novo acute myeloid leukaemia (ALFA-0701): a randomised, open-label, phase 3 study*. Lancet, 2012. 379(9825): pp. 1508–16.

Chapter 3

Introduction to Big Data in Education and Its Contribution to the Quality Improvement Processes

Christos Vaitsis, Vasilis Hervatis and Nabil Zary

Additional information is available at the end of the chapter

http://dx.doi.org/10.5772/63896

Abstract

In this chapter, we introduce the readers to the field of big educational data and how big educational data can be analysed to provide insights into different stakeholders and thereby foster data driven actions concerning quality improvement in education. For the analysis and exploitation of big educational data, we present different techniques and popular applied scientific methods for data analysis and manipulation such as analytics and different analytical approaches such as learning, academic and visual analytics, providing examples of how these techniques and methods could be used. The concept of quality improvement in education is presented in relation to two factors: (a) to improvement science and its impact on different processes in education such as the learning, educational and academic processes and (b) as a result of the practical application and realization of the presented analytical concepts. The context of health professions education is used to exemplify the different concepts.

Keywords: big data, big educational data, analytics, health education, quality improvement

1. Introduction

Higher and professional education is a domain which constantly needs to be evaluated and transformed to follow the fast pace of changing trends in different sectors in the market which in turn creates a variety of needs in workforce. A major factor that has radically altered the way education is conducted is technology. Examples of different types of technologies used in education are mobile devices and apparatuses, teleconference and remote access systems, educational platforms and services and other that students, teachers, academic faculty, evaluation specialists, researchers and decision-makers in education interact with and use in an effort to impact and improve teaching and learning but also to realistically reflect in the learning stage the usage of modern technologies used in real settings. The interaction with these technologies generates large amounts of data that range from an individual access log file to an institutional level activity. Still the educational systems are not yet fully prepared to cope with and exploit them for continuous quality improvement purposes. In particularly, health professions education or health education is a context that these technologies are predominantly used, producing a wide range of educational data. In addition, health education is in constant need of reflecting the growing body of medical knowledge and evidence in order to practically embed it in education and prepare the future health professionals to meet the future challenges of healthcare systems. The need to govern these challenges within health education is now more than ever timely, and therefore, attention has been paid to different approaches such as big data and analytics that could be useful in investigating and exploiting educational data too.

2. Big data and education

2.1. Big data

Big data is extensively used as a term today to describe and define the recent emergence and existence of data sets of high magnitude. It can be found in many sectors. The public, commercial and social sectors receive and produce ceaselessly vast amounts of data from different sources and in different formats. In some cases, the data reach extremely big sizes such as in petabytes exceeding the hardware or human abilities to warehouse, manipulate and process them and therefore is characterized as big data. Nevertheless, this term has been readily given to large sized data, although the size can vary from sector to sector or more specifically between services within a sector [1]. Big data is in fact termed as such given its characteristic of being large in size. Nevertheless, big data is defined by additional characteristics such as the disparate types and formats and different sources the data are collected from but also the speed they are produced, and most importantly, the frequency they are processed, in real time, frequently or occasionally. All these characteristics are summarized as volume (size), variety (sources, formats and types) and velocity (speed and frequency) and add complexity to the data, which is in fact another attribute in concern [2]. Data possessed in a system or a specific domain are considered as big data when simultaneously the volume, the variety and the velocity are high irrespective of whether these three characteristics can be considered "small" to another domain. In this case, this is enough to challenge constrains in manipulating and analysing the data so they can be used for different purposes. Depending on the domain, the size of data can vary from megabytes to petabytes. Thus, big data is context-specific and may refer to different sizes and types from domain to domain but the common challenge that all these domains must cope with is to being able to make sense of the data by processing them in a high analytical level to enable data-driven improvement of processes and procedures [3]. Big data and analytics have added value to data possessed in different contexts and consequently have proven to be an extremely useful approach for investigating its possible impact

http://dx.doi.org/10.5772/63896

either in industry in the form of business intelligence and analytics [4] or in academia with educational data mining techniques and learning analytics [5]. Given the limited research on the usage of big data and analytics in the context of health education, we will introduce the reader to the new field of big educational data which places big data in education and how the educational data can be treated in different dimensions and from different perspectives to bring into light insights for different stakeholders such as decision-makers, academic faculty, evaluation specialists, researchers and students in computer science, engineering and informatics courses and encourage accordingly data-driven activities concerning quality improvement in education.

2.2. Big educational data

One of the domains that volume, variety and velocity coexist in the data is the higher education. Large amounts of educational data are captured and generated on a daily basis from different sources and in different formats in the higher educational ecosystem. The educational data vary from those produced from students' usage and interaction with learning management systems (LMSs) and platforms, to learning activities and courses information consisting a curriculum such as learning objectives, syllabuses, learning material and activities, examination results and courses' evaluation, to other kind of data related to administrative, educational and quality improvement processes and procedures. The limited exploitation of big educational data and the size and type of these data within the context of higher education signifies the need for special techniques to be applied in order to discover new beneficial knowledge that currently is hidden within data [6]. Such techniques can be derived and adapted from other domains characterized by big data and successfully used to manipulate big educational data. These techniques could be used to enable the development of insights "regarding student performance and learning approaches" and exemplify areas within big educational data—such as students' actual performance according to taught curriculum—that can be positively impacted [7]. Recently, big data and Analytics together have shown promise in promoting different actions in higher education. These actions concern "administrative decision-making and organizational resource allocation", prevention of students at risk to fail by early identify them, development of effective instructional techniques and transform the traditional view of the curriculum to reconsider it as a network of relations and connections between the different entities of data gathered and regularly produced from LMSs, social networks, learning activities and the curriculum [8]. More specifically, one of the identified areas in which big data and Analytics are appropriately applicable for investigation and improvement in higher education is the curriculum and its contents, as a major part of big educational data [9, 10].

2.3. Big educational data in health education

Health education is an interesting context since it is complex. Its complexity lies in the constantly increased body of medical knowledge and evidence that continuously needs to be reflected in educational activities in order to match the needs for competent health professionals that meet the demands of the healthcare system and the society as its stakeholder. It produces an enormous amount of educational data considered as big. More specifically, the variety of data encased from teaching, learning and assessment activities, make it an area in which big data and analytics can be very useful to exploit them and sort out the complex information to be found in large diverse data sets [11]. Using big data and analytics techniques as an approach to make sense of the data, representing a health education curriculum and the associations between them, revealed its underlying complexity and the power that these techniques offer in two different cases.

In the first case [12], it was attempted to analyze and visualize the connections between the overall intended learning outcomes (ILO—in red) given in the different courses of an undergraduate medical curriculum and the desired competencies—from both the medical programme (in blue) and the higher education board (in dark and light green)—a medical student should have acquired after graduation from the medical programme. This is considered an attempt to make sense of this data in a small scale but yet, even in this case, the visualizations (**Figures 1** and **2**) reveal and confirm the high levels of complexity of this data. Further, considering as we mentioned before the continuously growing medical evidence that needs to realistically be reflected in the educational activities, the nature of this data is not static and represent only a snapshot of a long-term changeable network on the time it was captured. Yet, meaningful conclusions can be derived in a glance from these visualizations such as which competency is addressed the most with ILOs (connections between light green and red in **Figure 1**), or for example, clusters of ILOs used to address either knowledge or skills while addressing a common competency of the medical programme (connections between red non-clustered and clustered in **Figure 2**), and more.

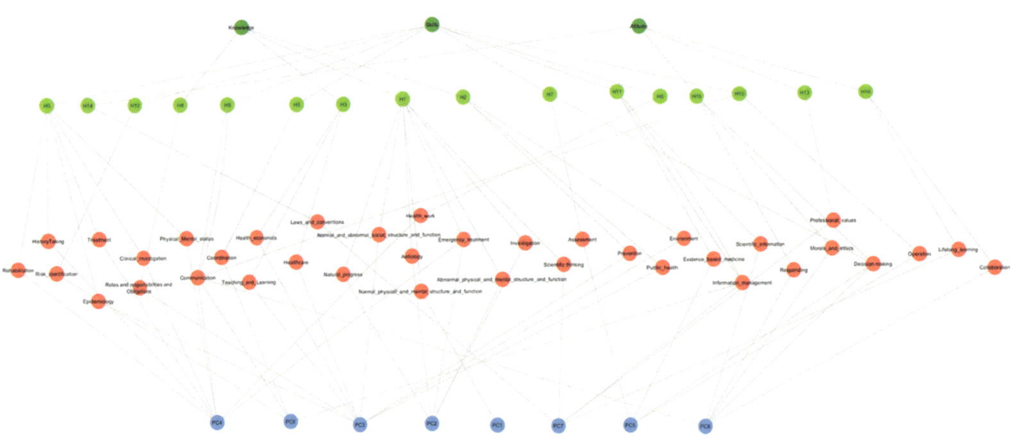

Figure 1. Competencies and ILOs map.

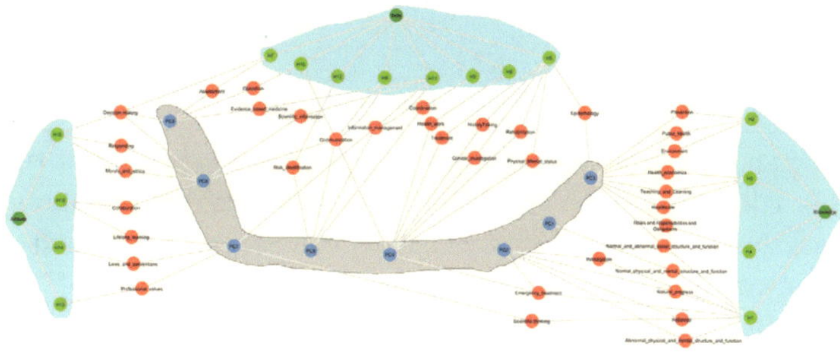

Figure 2. Clusters of competencies and ILOs.

In the second case [13], it was attempted to visualize in a global association map the connections created by the practical incorporation of MeSH terminology in one particular section of a medical curriculum (**Figure 3**). Again, despite the obvious complexity of the MeSH map, conclusions can easily be derived quickly concerning, for example the less often used MeSH terms, here depicted in small clusters and located outside the main big cluster. Of course, this kind of representations require considerable time to be processed by humans due to their high complexity, but definitely they can promote understanding of overview of the situation and facilitate high-level reporting of bulks of information.

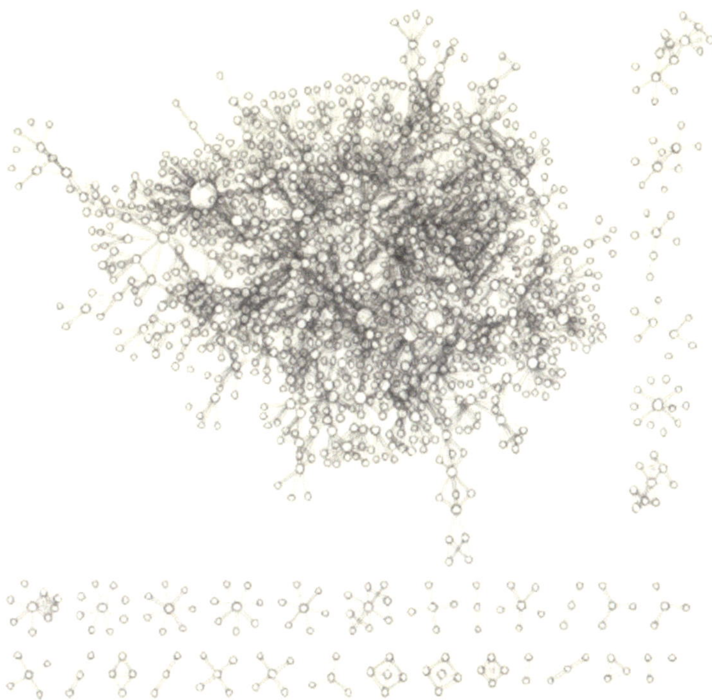

Figure 3. MeSH terms association map of a particular section of a medical curriculum.

3. Analytics

3.1. Dimensions and objectives

From a broad perspective, the development of analytics models has shown promise in transforming big educational data in health education into an Analytics-driven quality management tool. In the world of academic and learning analytics, the sources that big educational data are derived from are distinguished in different levels. This gives a multidisciplinary character to the field of analytics in general, involving various techniques, methods and approaches frequently used in the field. The range of actions that can be taken within the analytics area is wide, and frequently, these actions are classified into different levels and dimensions. For instance, the different actions taken in the field are divided by some practitioners into three different dimensions: time, level and stakeholder. Specific analytical approaches are applied to address respective questions for each of the dimensions. Descriptive analytics, for instance, produces reports, summaries and models in the dimension of time to answer the what, how and why something did happen. It monitors also processes to provide alerts in real time and recommend answers to questions as: What is happening now? In the case of predictive analytics, past actions are evaluated to estimate the future actions outcomes by answering: What are the trends, and what is likely to happen. It also simulates alternative actions outcomes to support decisions. Using analytics, choices are based on evidence rather than assumptions [14].

Analytics has been also classified into five levels: course, department, institution, region and national/international [8]. Other terms attempting to define the different levels more specifically can be applied; "nanolevel" indicates activities in a course; the "microlevel" points an entire course in an education programme; the "mesolevel" includes many courses in a specific academic year; and finally, the "macrolevel" concerns many study programmes in an educational institution [15]. **Figure 4** shows these four levels and the relation between them.

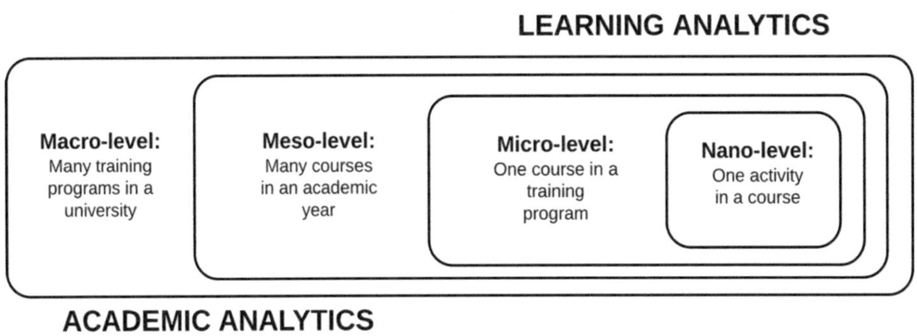

Figure 4. Overlapping of Analytics levels in higher education.

When the focus is on decision-making concerning achievements of specific learning outcomes, then all included actions are governed by "learning analytics" which refers to operations at the microlevel and nanolevel. When the focus is on decision-making regarding procedures, management and matters of operational nature, then it is governed by "academic analytics" which applies to the other two levels, macro and meso [16]. **Figure 4** illustrates how the different levels of analytics in education overlap and complement each other. For example, results of actions taken in the nanolevel can be input to the other levels micro, meso and macro, while it is controlled and monitored by them. The application of analytics in this classification can also be oriented toward different stakeholders, including students, teachers, administrators, institutions, and researchers. They may have different objectives, such as mentoring, monitoring, analysis, prediction, assessment, feedback, personalization, recommendation, and decision support. Despite the categorization of analytics actions in different levels, the data that these levels generate enter the same analytics loop which is defined in five steps in **Table 1** [17].

Steps	Description
Step 1: capture	Data are the foundation of all analytics. These data can be produced by different systems and stored in multiple databases. One great challenge for analytics projects in this step is that necessary data may be missing, stored in multiple formats or hidden in shadow systems
Step 2: report	Dashboards provide an overview of trends or correlations. This step involves creating an overview to scan. Different tools can be used to create queries, examine information and identify trends and patterns. Descriptive statistics and dashboards can be used to graphically visualize eventual correlations
Step 3: predict	Predictions and probabilities can be derived. Different tools can be used to apply predictive models. Typically, these models are based on statistical regression. Different regression techniques are available and each one has limitations
Step 4: act	The goal of analytics is to provide actionable insights through information based on predictions and probabilities that support decision making. Analytics can be used to evaluate past actions and estimate the effects of future actions. In that way, analytics can provide alternative actions and simulate the consequences of different actions
Step 5: refine	The evaluation feeding back the self-improvement. The monitoring, feedback and evaluation of the project's impact create new data and evidence that can be used to start the loop again with improved performance

Table 1. Steps in analytics loop.

Another type of classification was proposed [18] and provides a division in different dimensions: The environment; what data is available? The stakeholders; who is targeted? The objectives; why do the analysis? And the method; how has the analysis been performed? Finally, analytics can team up with other scientific areas for analysis and high-level communication of actions such as scientific information visualization and data analysis techniques (e.g. data mining and network analysis) elaborated upon later in Section 3.2.4 in the chapter.

3.2. Analytical approaches

As we saw, there are different components that analytics actions need in order to be effective. These components are the data (type and source) and the context in interest. If these components of analytics are in place, we are able to create different analytics models which can thrive and grow into an analytics engine capable to harness big educational data to ultimately contribute to the quality management and improvement of health education. Based each time on the needs of the health educational ecosystem in question, different approaches can result in building multiple viewpoint analytical models. The analytics approaches presented below are not specifically related to any type of classification in dimensions or levels but rather can work with any type of analytics model which constitutes all necessary components.

3.2.1. Data-driven analytics approach

Reading from the left to the right, **Figure 5** describes the common and traditional data-driven analytics approach, which is quite meaningful to experts in the data analysis area. It starts from the data and ends in the decision. The main focus is on the data and the necessary techniques to collect, store, clean, secure, transfer and process them. According to this approach, the loop starts in the first step by capturing as much data as possible, and then, the data are pushed through the different steps. Into the reporting step, the high volume of data is an asset. The more data we add, the better results we will receive. However, processing massive data sets includes challenges, such as demand for high-level mining techniques and more robust computers, applications, software and skills. To make sense of all this data, estimate the trends and examine all possible associations is a challenging task. Data analysis techniques, necessary to process the data in this step, require expertise usually found in data analysts and most commonly within the educational data mining area. Based on the evidence from previous steps, the engine predicts the trends and suggests actions that might be accurate and precise, but still remain suggestions. Often, the decision makers, frequently because of unknown circumstances, underestimate the recommendations and act differently. The loop finishes with the last step which is to either end the loop or feed the engine with more data in step 1 and run the engine again.

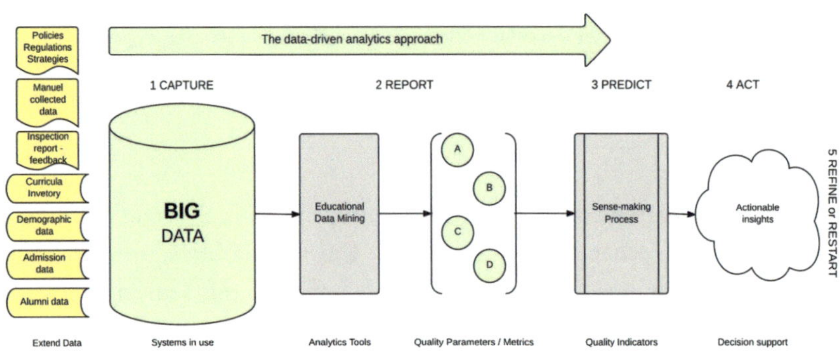

Figure 5. Data-driven Analytics Approach.

http://dx.doi.org/10.5772/63896

3.2.2. *Context- or need-driven analytics approach*

The model reads also from backwards (steps 1–8 in **Figure 6**). It describes in this way a new analytics approach called context- or need-driven analytics. This approach is more suitable for less qualified group of users in data analysis techniques such as educators and decision-makers. The approach starts from the need for a decision and goes through the analysis of relevant data which could support the decisions. Quality improvements, decisions and actions must be crystal clear. Every detail is important: the stakeholders, the circumstances, particular needs, economic boundaries, accessibility of resources, organizational atmosphere, policies, technological ecosystem, timing and other factors which could influence the decisions. The results of this investigation are the demands of specific information to support a judgment or micro-decisions. This important and particular information emerges from the integration of carefully picked and explicit data. These data are selected, prepared, assessed, compared and produced by analytics tools utilizing particular mining methods. The analytics engine includes additional mechanisms and specific operators to recognize the systems which generate the data or the containers which carry the data. This time, we extract just the necessary data we need. Finally, the analytics loop either filter the data and provide an answer to the primary question or re-enter a new, more precise, question and restart the analytics process [19].

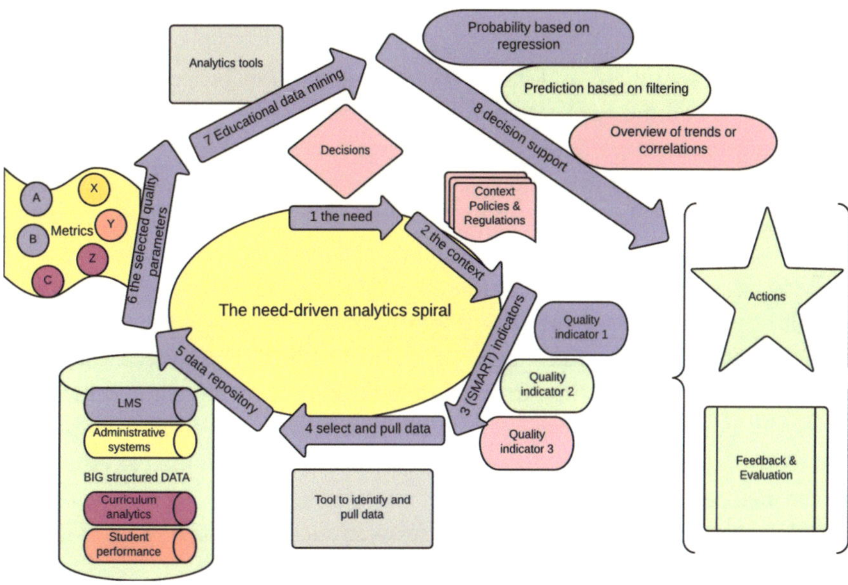

Figure 6. Context- or need-driven Analytics Approach.

3.3. Learning analytics

The term "learning analytics (LA)" is defined as "the measurement, collection, analysis and reporting of data about learners and their contexts, for purposes of understanding and optimising learning and the environments in which it occurs" [20] and affects actions and operations at the microlevel and nanolevel in **Figure 4**. Through LA, we can detect similarities in behaviours (e.g. user's satisfaction) or detect anomalous patterns (e.g. cheating). It can function as a bridge between past and future operations by inserting data concerning past events into a LA engine and analyse them to determine the probable future outcomes. It can synthesize thus big educational data and create a set of predictions to suggest different decision options revealing each time the implications of each decision option. LA can be further enhanced through visuals to amplify insight, increase understanding and impact decision-making as we explain further, later in the chapter.

Teachers, usually based on their experience, use their own "gut feeling" to translate students' behaviour and suspect if a student might drop out of a course or even abandon the studies. This can be proven to be either true or false, but without evidence, there is low level of certainty in decisions that are based only on experience. An example demonstrates the LA capacity to use evidence and add confidence to this type of decisions [21]. Here, data mining techniques were applied in big educational data and were utilized as a part of an analytics engine to detect students that perform in high, middle and low levels and notify them accordingly with different types of feedback. Thus, students at risk were identified very early when the institution still had the time to react and take preventive actions.

3.4. Academic analytics

The term "academic analytics" is defined as "the intersection of technology, information, management culture and the application of information to manage the academic enterprise" [22] and affects actions and operations at the macro and mesolevel as we saw before in **Figure 4**. The focus of academic analytics includes reporting, modelling, analysis and decision support concerning university and campus services. Examples of this kind of services include, but not limited to admission, advising, financing, academic counselling, enrolment and administration. Following is a practical use of academic analytics [23], where librarians have used analytics on library usage data as part of the big educational data ecosystem to predict students' grades demonstrating the value that can be provided by the data produced and processed in the library to the hosting institution. In another case [24], it is demonstrated how within the context of health education academic analytics reports extracted from a mapped medical curriculum using data mining techniques, can add transparency to the big educational data consisting the medical curriculum and can be of use to stakeholders to facilitate decisions that need to be taken concerning different kinds of services such as managerial and financial.

3.5. Visual analytics

Methods and techniques have been developed in the recent years that can be used to manipulate complicated data in many different disciplines [25, 26]. Visual analytics (VA) is the science of analytical reasoning supported by interactive visual interfaces as an outgrowth of the fields of information visualization and scientific visualization [27]. VA combines different techniques: information visualization, data analysis and the power of human visual perception (**Figure 7**) [28].

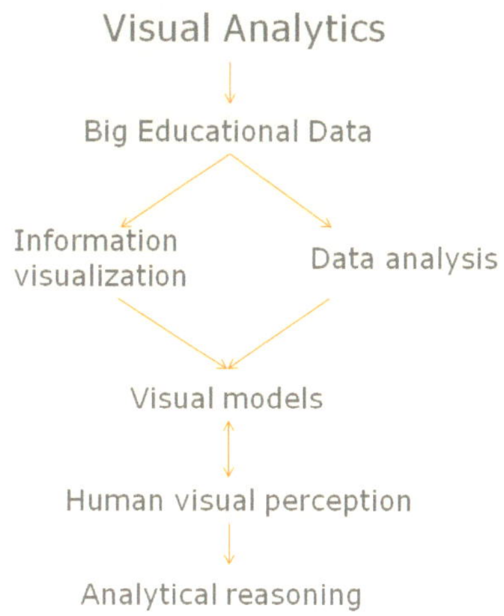

Figure 7. Big educational data are modelled by information visualization and data analysis techniques and represented in visual interfaces with which the human visual perception interacts to impact the analytical reasoning process.

It has the potential to support in the process of manipulating big data and exploit them by creating a holistic view of the data while revealing underlying complex information to the extent possible to positively impact analytical reasoning and decision-making [29–31]. A review of the literature resulted in identifying variables [32, 33] that are able to support analytical reasoning and decision making through VA and the interaction between human visual perception and visual interfaces as below:

- Increased cognitive resources (V1)
- Decreased need to search for information (V2)
- Enhancement of the recognition of patterns (V3)
- Easier perception of inference of relationships (V4)
- Increased ability to explore and manipulate the data (V5)

The potentials offered by VA making it a promising tool to explore also how big educational data could contribute to the quality improvement of higher education. Different approaches prove the potential of VA to impact quality improvement specifically within the context of health education. It is reported [34] how the analysis and a simple visualization of educational data of a medical programme enabled involved stakeholders to instantly review and preview the effects of implemented changes in a medical curriculum. We will examine how in another case, VA has been practically used to explore its impact on analytical reasoning and decision making using big educational data from a medical programme [35, 36].

In **Figure 8**, we see how the learning outcomes (LO) and the teaching methods (TM) of one course were modelled to visually represent the hidden underlying network of connections and relations between them. The TMs are depicted in percentages in red, to show to what extent each TM is used in the course out of a 100%. Each TM addresses a number of LOs, and these are depicted in light blue. The percentages between an individual TM and its LOs depict the extent in which each TM's content is used to address the specific LO. A number of non-addressed LOs are depicted on the top-right corner to complete the set of predefined LOs (16 in total) that the medical programme should address within the different courses. Here, the LOs and TMs are mapped and represented hierarchically from its 100% of TMs to corresponding percentages of TMs showing to which extent each TM is used in the course. Going further, the percentages between TMs and LOs reveal how much of the learning content of the TM is used to address the specific LO. For instance, the "clinical training" TM is fully addressing LO7 with its learning content while uses only 10% (5% out of 50%) of the learning content to address LO8. Thus, a comparison between learning content usage can instantly show which LO is mostly addressed and reveal the tendency of the TM or even the whole course—when we compare all TMs—towards specific LOs and even further competencies build through the LOs. This approach provides a way of analysing the teaching part of the course in relation to the LOs addressed to support the process of analytical reasoning. In the event of a series of similar comparisons, an instructor can base its decisions concerning the right percentage to address an LO and reform and redesign accordingly if necessary, to be more tailored to the LO's importance. In this way, an instructor evaluates and confirms the correct usage of TMs to address the LOs even if redesigning is not necessary. In parallel, a comparison between addressed and non-addressed LOs and between used and non-used TMs can be performed at any moment, revealing the whole course's map.

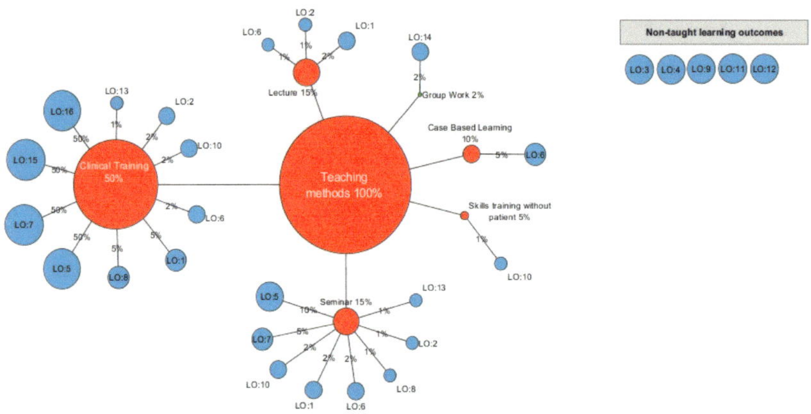

Figure 8. Learning outcomes and teaching methods.

In **Figure 9**, we see how the LOs of the same course were modelled this time against the assessment part and more specifically one part of the assessment, the questions used in the written examination, 34 in total. The percentages on the connections between yellow and red circles depict the proportion (out of 100%) of exam questions used to address the specific LO in red. For instance, eleven questions are used to assess LO5 which corresponds to 32%. Groups of LOs correspond to main outcomes—knowledge, skills and attitude—which are depicted in green. In cases where multiple main outcomes are assessed in groups of questions, the total

http://dx.doi.org/10.5772/63896

percentage is divided into single main outcomes as in the case where 30% of the questions are used to assess skills and knowledge corresponding to 15% skills and 15% knowledge. An instant observation is that 83% of the questions on the written examination are used to assess skills, while 16% are used to assess knowledge and 1% attitude. Also, the percentage of questions that assess each of the LOs reveals how the written examination is built around them and which LOs are most heavily assessed. Some LOs are assessed in more than one group of questions, like LO5 in five different cases with corresponding red circles or in combination with other learning outcomes, like LO7 in two cases. The analytical process is supported in this case by instantly evaluating how the LOs of the course are assessed in the written examination. The percentages of questions can be examined against the importance of the assessed LO and thus suggest whether it is the correct percentage of questions, compared to the other percentages of questions used to assess other LOs. Thus, an instructor can decide if these percentages should be adjusted according to the importance of LOs and redesign the questions of the examination or even if it is more appropriate to address these LOs in other types of examination. Finally, this approach can be used to construct a more outcome-oriented written examination by redesigning it to cover identified gaps in addressing important LOs and instantly evaluating it with the updated visual model of the assessment activity.

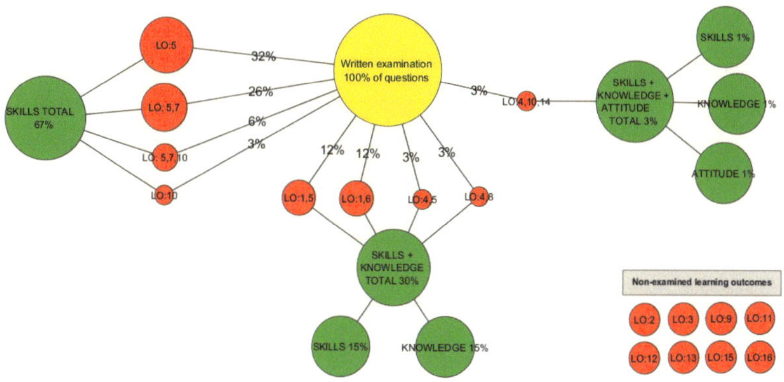

Figure 9. Examination and learning outcomes.

In **Figure 10**, we see an overview of the whole course. The TMs are depicted in red, main outcomes in yellow and LOs in light blue. The total points a student can get from each exam question are depicted inside the orange circles, and the percentages on the connections between these circles to LOs show the average success rate from all student answers on this particular question. The three light blue circles bordered in black (LO4,5, LO4,8 and LO4,10,14) and LO4 in bottom right corner depict the different cases where LO4 it is assessed by exam questions, but it is not taught in any of the TMs. This visualization sums all the information from Figures 9 and 10 providing additionally more information about the course in one place. Here, we can observe and analyse the entire course from different perspectives but also as a whole. Examining this figure from left to right and vice versa, different paths are created to disclose the underlying network in the examined educational data. The most focused and most assessed LOs can be observed instantly, showing the trend of the course towards skills, knowledge and attitude, to what extent these are addressed and if there are any gaps of taught/non-assessed LOs. Finally, the existence or not of the constructive alignment [37] in the course can be verified as a synthesis of possible identified gaps and the utilization of learning activities and LOs in one place presenting the course as a structured network.

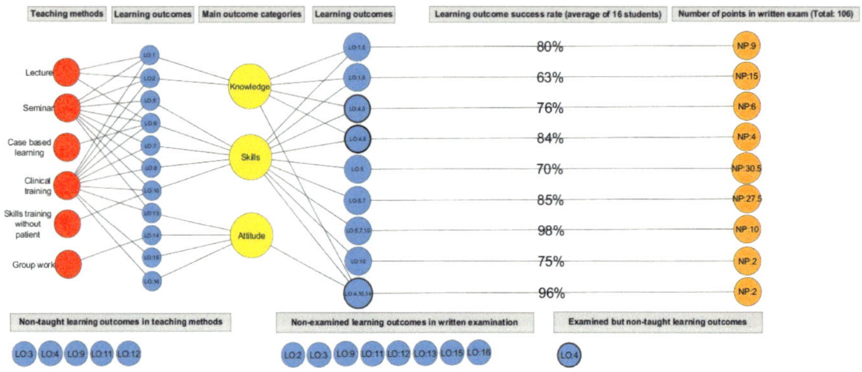

Figure 10. Overview of a course.

The analytical reasoning process is here more enhanced. The entire course can be instantly evaluated for gaps between taught and assessed LOs. For example, the identified gap for LO4 means simply that the written exam questions assess the LO4, but it was never actually taught in any of the TMs. This approach can be used as a tool in the hands of the course stakeholders to analyse it for this type of inconsistencies and possibly redesign it to establish a connection between what it is taught and what it is assessed and verify it again. After the redesigning, a comparison can take place where the different versions of the course will be similarly depicted before applying the desired changes in reality and thus create a more concrete and aligned course without gaps that meets the desired LOs appropriately.

The three presented approaches of using VA on big educational data within the context of health education demonstrate the potentials on impacting analytical reasoning and decision making in connection to the previously identified variables (V1–V5). Specifically, the information depicted is easily recognizable to the stakeholders in interest while making perceptible the different patterns and relations between the data (V1, V3 and V4). Searching for information relevant to the course structure is facilitated to a high extent (V2). The course can be readily analysed for gaps of different kinds while, at any time, the constructive alignment of the course can be verified (V3–V5). Finally, **Figure 10** has been further investigated with the use of augmented reality (AR) technology in an attempt to increase interactivity between the user and the visual and to enrich it with additional information while sustaining the complexity in low levels showing promising results for investigating big educational data by combining VA and AR [38].

http://dx.doi.org/10.5772/63896

4. Quality improvement (QI)

4.1. Quality improvement as an implication of improvement science in education

Quality improvement is defined as "the combined and unceasing efforts of everyone to make the changes that will lead to better outcomes, better system performance and better professional development" [39]. This definition covers all different aspects of health care that inextricably are affected by efforts targeting change. Improvement science instruments all the different ingredients and components necessary to realize this type of efforts that quality improvement requires to be a successful process. Improvement science has been applied in many disciplines such as automobile manufacturing and health care like an alternative approach to bring new knowledge into practice. Projects rooted in improvement science began to show success even within education. The characteristic of the improvement science is the holistic view of the examined context, and the key step is to identify the context (e.g. the organization, the actors and stakeholders, the routines and the workflow) and consider it as a system; deep knowledge of how small changes in a system instance can affect other parts of the system is very important.

Traditionally, improvement science was based on the "plan-do-study-act" cycle [40] attempting to answer fundamental questions such as:

- What are we trying to accomplish with the desired change?
- What changes can we make to achieve an improvement?
- How will we know that a change is also an improvement?

Today, the use of analytics in big educational data can be the "game changer" and can play an undeniably significant role in orchestrating the components of improvement science actions to design changes that successfully lead in improvement in the quality of education. Below is a formula that utilizes big educational data and combines the necessary components along with analytics within the context of education to successfully make a desired change to produce improvement.

4.2. The formula and its elements

The formula illustrates the way in which the different components come together like building blocks to produce improvement and can be used like a guide to design the change.

1	2	3	4	5
Context	+	Actionable Intelligence	→	Improvement

Each of the five elements is driven by a different knowledge area and has its own characteristics and settings.

4.2.1. Element #1: context

Deep knowledge of the particular context is the starting point. Differences on who, when, why, where and what can affect the choices we have or the selections we make. Different stakeholders perceive and use the terms and concepts differently in different occasions, but there are predominantly two ways to describe the context of education and define its quality. Some describe it as the personal development in people focusing on the outcome. They talk about "learning" and consider students like collaborators, or participants. Others describe education as the service of educating people focusing on the process. This group talks about "teaching" and considers the students like stakeholders, receivers, target group or customers/clients. Based on how we describe what education is we use different indicators to define its quality [41].

4.2.2. Element #2: the "+" symbol

This element represents the knowledge required about the different modalities for appropriate management of big educational data (analytics and data processing techniques) to properly connect and transform the context knowledge into the next element, the actionable intelligence.

4.2.3. Element #3: actionable intelligence

Through analytics, we can transform data to actionable insights and support decisions. As we have demonstrated, different analytics types, approaches and techniques are available (learning analytics, visual analytics, academic analytics, sense-making or predictive analytics, data-driven or need-driven analytics, etc.). Making decisions based on big educational data collected from complex learning environments may encounter limitations of human cognitive capability. That makes it necessary to expand this field and further investigate how different processes like cognitive artefacts that model human thinking sub-processes (e.g. accommodation, conclusions and categorization) could possibly facilitate the flow of human reasoning and therefore enhance the human cognitive ability [42, 43]. According to multiple analytics reports derived from the same data set, each of which provides a lens that adds more contextual insight will enable, for example the course developers to look for patterns [44, 45]. It is obvious that in our case the used final set of analytical reports as well as the selection between the mass univariate and multidimensional approach will emerge mostly from the available data sources and the technical/ethical possibilities to fuse them. Very often, the measures or parameters presented to the course developers will have to be extracted from the raw data with techniques, such as natural language processing, social network analysis, process mining and other.

4.2.4. Element #4: the → symbol

This element represents the knowledge about the execution and management of the change. The knowledge area is based on the Implementation Science and focuses on the methods and techniques required to "make things happen" and drive a successful implementation of an intervention in place.

http://dx.doi.org/10.5772/63896

4.2.5. Element #5: improvement

Improvement is about changing but not all changes are improvement. This element represents knowledge about the types and methods required to evaluate special types of measurements to show whether improvement has happened and calculate its impact. There are five different approaches depending on how we consider or view the quality [44] summarized in **Table 2**.

Quality is	Approach to measure
Exceptional; quality is something special	We create objectives, checking against standards and try to achieve "high class" or "excellence". This approach allows comparisons or benchmarking
Perfection or consistency; zero defects	In this approach, a service is judged by its consistency and reliability. The focus is on the processes to ensure that faults do not occur
Fitness for purpose; specification/mission and satisfaction	This approach is remote from the others. We accept that quality has meaning only in relation to the purpose and the users/stakeholders. It requires identification of the needs, continues monitoring, periodical re-evaluations and responsive adjustments
Value for money; Performance	This approach uses the terms "efficiency and effectiveness" and focuses on the accountability and linkage of the outcomes to the costs
Transformation; added value and empowering of the user	In this approach, we consider students as participants (not as products, customers, consumers, users or clients). In this case, education is an ongoing process of transformation of the participant and not a service for a customer

Table 2. The different approaches we follow for each one of the views.

4.3. Quality improvement of learning process

Operations at the microlevel and nanolevel (**Figure 4**) such as teaching or learning activities in a course are referred to LA. Examples of these operations are performed by teachers, course designers, studies and programme directors. The following scenario demonstrates the practical use of LA in the quality improvement circle of a course.

In the preparation phase of a course, the instructors can use curriculum mapping tools to discover actual gaps precisely. They can recognize thus which learning objectives are not properly addressed by teaching or learning activities. They need recommendations for new, more proper and motivational teaching activities to include them into their schedule. With the available Analytics tools, they are able to analyse further the class and predict its needs such as student demographics, performance, different learning approaches, the technology used and the group dynamics. This type of data is processed by a number of algorithms and predictive models that can develop the characteristics of the class [32]. Visualization tools can be used for the following round to give alternative proposals for designing suitable activities fitting this particular class and also illustrate the effects of each of the options. The course director can control the activities and observe students' progress during the ongoing course. They can zoom in and out from the whole class to one working group or one individual student. They can additionally track the flow of the formed social networks. They can judge the overall commitment and identify students at risk. In an extensively used platform, they can also compare particular indicators from other classes, or through to other anonymized data sets within the same program, or from a different department, or even compare against data from related programs in other universities [46]. The results and the produced experiences can be used to build up the knowledge database evidently regarding several pedagogical interventions. This can support in forming new policies in the entire organization and be an important element of the quality development and academic research.

4.4. Quality improvement of educational process

We presented how VA could be used to support the analytical reasoning and decision making of stakeholders involved in the quality improvement of the educational process. This is achieved when both visual and analytics factors function as instruments of a harmonized engine that complement and support each other. The analytics factor applied on the big educational data aims at reducing its complexity without losing vital information and critical characteristics; these are kept at the top level of the presented visuals. The other factor is the visualization, which brought pathways and relations into light by taking advantage of the human ability to process and understand visual information more easily. These two factors cannot stand alone without each other and be implemented to data with incoherent structure, which makes Analytics an essential key component to build a strong base for a meaningful VA result. The data analysis preceding visualizations assists in shaping the inchoate big educational data that visuals are then responsible to represent. An important point is the effort needed to apply each of the factors. The effort required for the visual and analytics parts is not comparable, and their roles are totally different. Analytics requires significant effort to shape the data in question and compile all the discrete elements to represent the data adequately. On the contrary, visuals require less effort since the network of connections and relations is already assembled. However, to select and gradually build the appropriate visuals, it requires expertise in order to emphasize in a big picture the essential information existing in the network produced from data analysis and add scientific value onto it while going beyond simple statistical-based visuals. Of course, the human visual perception is irreplaceable in this chain of actions in order to perceive and interact with the visual interfaces and perform high-level analysis. In summary, VA allows the different stakeholders to easily perceive the structure of the examined data, define how each part coexists as part of a network and reason for its use and importance in the data. It also helps to better understand stakeholders' individual role in the educational process and the consequences of delivering their parts without being able to determine how it can be harmonized with other parts in the data. It supports stakeholders also to decide how to cope with discrepancies and structure anomalies revealed from gap analysis and the existence or not of the constructive alignment in the data. Finally, VA can display currently needed changes for an improved future overall picture in order to deliver health education in pace with healthcare demands [47, 48]. Revealing the underlying network of information in the examined data, identifying gaps, discrepancies and anomalies between the data and being able to verify the appropriateness of the given educational activities promotes the process of analytical reasoning and decision making and transforms the big educational data into an instrument for planning and applying changes in a constant effort for quality improvement in health education.

4.5. Quality improvement of academic functions and campus services

Academic analytics has been compared to business intelligence and refers to operations at the macrolevel and mesolevel as we saw in **Figure 4**, including decision support concerning university and campus services. In most of the cases, Academic Analytics have been used to provide actionable insights and support single or isolated decisions [49]. As we demonstrated Academic Analytics is a main part of the quality improvement process and can be beneficial in multiple ways into the steps of the improvement's cycle. Into the early steps of the cycle (the data-driven approach, **Figure 5**), it can support decision makers to identify the gaps and the needs of what is possible or necessary to improve. Into the following steps, academic analytics can support decision about choosing appropriate actions trough predictions and by providing "what if" scenarios using the need-driven approach in **Figure 6**. Academic analytics (through dashboards and reports) can be used to monitor the ongoing processes and support decisions concerning eventual adjustments. At the end of the quality improvement cycle, academic analytics can support in performing evaluations of the intervention's impact demonstrating the hidden connections between actions and events.

5. Conclusion

The goal of this chapter was to introduce the reader to the concept of big educational data and the different forms of analytics as applied scientific areas and go deeper to popular techniques for data manipulation and how they can be transferred within the health education system and used as approaches to exploit big educational data that such systems produce. Apart from the techniques itself, the benefits and potential to use them for quality improvement purposes in health education are provided and discussed in detail.

In the era of technology and its inevitable impact on health education systems, such approaches are proven to be quite utilitarian in order to support the quality improvement process of education and ultimately contribute to health care with highly skilled health professionals.

Acknowledgements

We wish to thank all the staff at Karolinska Institutet, Sweden that provided the authors of this chapter with assistance, comments and encouragement.

Author details

Christos Vaitsis[1*], Vasilis Hervatis[1] and Nabil Zary[1,2]

*Address all correspondence to: christos.vaitsis@ki.se

1 Department of Learning, Informatics, Management and Ethics, Karolinska Institutet, Stockholm, Sweden

2 Lee Kong Chian School of Medicine, Nanyang Technological University, Singapore, Singapore

References

[1] Manyika J, Chui M, Brown B, Bughin J, Dobbs R, Roxburgh C, Byers AH. "Big Data: The Next Frontier for Innovation, Competition, and Productivity," McKinsey Global Institute; San Francisco. 2011.

[2] Zaslavsky A, Perera C, Georgakopoulos D. Sensing as a service and big data. arXiv preprint. 2013;1301.0159.

[3] Zikopoulos P, Eaton C. Understanding Big Data: Analytics for Enterprise Class Hadoop and Streaming Data. McGraw-Hill Osborne Media; New York. 2011.

[4] Chen H, Chiang RH, Storey VC. Business intelligence and analytics: from Big Data to Big Impact. MIS Quarterly. 2012;36(4):1165–88.

[5] Baker RS, Inventado PS. Educational data mining and learning analytics. In: Larusson A. J., White B. editors. Learning Analytics, Springer, New York. 2014; 61–75.

[6] Romero C, Ventura S. Educational data mining: a survey from 1995 to 2005. Expert Systems with Applications. 2007;33(1):135–46.

[7] West DM. Big data for education: data mining, data analytics, and web dashboards. Governance Studies at Brookings. 2012;4:1–0.

[8] Siemens G, Long P. Penetrating the Fog: Analytics in Learning and Education. EDUCAUSE Review. 2011;46(5):30.

[9] Picciano AG. The Evolution of Big Data and Learning Analytics in American Higher Education. Journal of Asynchronous Learning Networks. 2012;16(3):9–20.

[10] Komenda M, Schwarz D, Vaitsis C, Zary N, Štěrba J, Dušek L. OPTIMED Platform: curriculum harmonisation system for medical and healthcare education. Studies in Health Technology and Informatics. 2015;210:511.

[11] Ellaway RH, Pusic MV, Galbraith RM, Cameron T. Developing the role of big data and analytics in health professional education. Medical Teacher. 2014;36(3):216–22.

[12] Vaitsis C, Nilsson G, Zary N. Big data in medical informatics: improving education through visual analytics. Studies in Health Technology in Informatics. 2014;205:1163–7.

[13] Komenda M, Schwarz D, Švancara J, Vaitsis C, Zary N, Dušek L. Practical use of medical terminology in curriculum mapping. Computers in Biology and Medicine. 2015;63:74–82.

[14] Cooper A. A brief history of Analytics. JISC CETIS Analytics Series. 2012;1(9):1–21

[15] Mendez G, Ochoa X, Chiluiza K, de Wever B. Curricular design analysis: a data-driven perspective. Journal of Learning Analytics. 2014;1(3):84–119.

[16] van Barneveld A, Arnold KE, Campbell JP. Analytics in higher education: establishing a common language. EDUCAUSE Learning Initiative. 2012;1:1–1.

[17] Campbell JP, DeBlois PB, Oblinger DG. Academic analytics. EDUCAUSE Review. 2007;42(10):40–57

[18] Chatti MA, Dyckhoff AL, Schroeder U, Thüs H. A reference model for learning analytics. International Journal of Technology Enhanced Learning. 2012;4(5–6):318–31.

[19] Hervatis V, Loe A, Barman L, O'Donoghue J, Zary N. A conceptual analytics model for an outcome-driven quality management framework as part of professional healthcare education. JMIR Medical Education. 2015;1(2):e11.

[20] Siemens G. 1st International Conference on Learning Analytics and Knowledge. Connecting the technical, pedagogical, and social dimensions of learning analytics [Internet]. 2011. Available from: https://tekri.athabascau.ca/analytics/ [Accessed 2016-05-26]

[21] Tanes Z, Arnold KE, King AS, Remnet MA. Using signals for appropriate feedback: perceptions and practices. Computers & Education. 2011;57(4):2414–22.

[22] Goldstein PJ, Katz RN. Academic Analytics: The Use of Management Information and Technology in Higher Education—Key Findings. Boulder, CO: Educause Center for Applied Research. 2005.

[23] Cox B, Jantti M. Discovering the Impact of Library Use and Student Performance EDUCAUSE Review. [Internet]. 2012 Available from: http://www.educause.edu/ero/article/discovering-impact-library-use-and-student-performance [Accessed 2016-05-26]

[24] Komenda M, Víta M, Vaitsis C, Schwarz D, Pokorná A, Zary N, Dušek L. Curriculum Mapping with Academic Analytics in Medical and Healthcare Education. PloS One. 2015;10(12):e0143748

[25] Perer A. Finding Beautiful Insights in the Chaos of Social Network Visualization. In: Steele J, Iliinsky N, editors. Beautiful Visualization. Looking at Data Through the Eyes of Experts. O'Reilly Media; Beijing; 2010; pp. 157–73.

[26] Witten I, Frank EH, Hall MA. Data Mining. Practical Machine Learning Tools and Techniques. 3rd ed. Morgan Kaufmann Series in Data Management Systems; Burlington; 2011; pp. 375–97.

[27] Thomas J., Cook K. Illuminating the Path: Research and Development Agenda for Visual Analytics. IEEE-Press. 2005.

[28] Visual Analytics portal [Internet]. Available from: http://www.visual-Analytics.eu/ [Accessed: 2016-03-17]

[29] Keim DA, Mansmann F, Thomas J. Visual analytics: how much visualization and how much analytics? ACM SIGKDD Explorations Newsletter. 2010;11(2):5–8.

[30] Steed C, Potok T, Patton R, Goodall J, Maness C, Senter J. Interactive Visual Analysis of High Throughput Text Streams. In: Proceedings of The 2nd Workshop on Interactive Visual Text Analytics, Oct 15, 2012, Seattle, WA, USA [Internet]. 2012. Available from: http://aser.ornl.gov/publications_2013/Publication 39367.pdf [Accessed 2016-05-26]

[31] Keim DA, Mansmann F, Stoffel A, Ziegler H. Visual Analytics. Encyclopedia of Database Systems. Springer, New York. 2009; pp. 3341–3346.

[32] Mazza R. Visualization in educational environments. In: Romero C, Ventura S, Pechenizkiy M, Baker RSJD. editors. Handbook of Educational Data Mining. 1st ed. Chapman & Hall/CRC Data Mining and Knowledge Discovery Series, London. 2010. pp. 9–27

[33] Card SK, Mackinlay JD, Shneiderman B. Readings in information visualization: using vision to think. Morgan Kaufmann, Burlington. 1999.

[34] Olmos M, Corrin L. Academic analytics in a medical curriculum: Enabling educational excellence. Australasian Journal of Educational Technology. 2012;28(1):1–5.

[35] Vaitsis C, Nilsson G, Zary N. Visual analytics in healthcare education: exploring novel ways to analyze and represent big data in undergraduate medical education. PeerJ. 2014;2:e683.

[36] Vaitsis C, Nilsson G, Zary N. Visual Analytics in Medical Education: Impacting Analytical Reasoning and Decision Making for Quality Improvement. Studies in Health Technology and Informatics. 2015;210:95.

[37] Biggs JB. Teaching for Quality Learning at University: What the Student Does. McGraw-Hill Education, New York. 2011.

[38] Nifakos S, Vaitsis C, Zary N. AUVA-augmented reality empowers visual analytics to explore medical curriculum data. Studies in Health Technology and Informatics. 2015;210:494.

http://dx.doi.org/10.5772/63896

[39] Batalden PB, Davidoff F. What is "quality improvement" and how can it transform healthcare? Quality and Safety in Health Care. 2007;16(1):2–3.

[40] Lewis C. What is improvement science? Do We Need It in Education?. Educational Researcher. 2015;44(1):54–61.

[41] Barrett AM, Chawla-Duggan R, Lowe J, Nikel J, Ukpo E. The Concept of Quality in Education: A Review of the "International" Literature on the Concept of Quality in Education. England: EdQual. 2006.

[42] Green TM, Ribarsky W. Using a human cognition model in the creation of collaborative knowledge visualizations. InSPIE Defense and Security Symposium. International Society for Optics and Photonics. 2008;69830C.

[43] Green TM, Ribarsky W, Fisher B. Visual analytics for complex concepts using a human cognition model. In: IEEE Symposium on Visual Analytics Science and Technology; 19–24 October 2008; Columbus, OH; p. 91–98.

[44] Harvey L, Knight PT. Transforming Higher Education. Open University Press, Taylor & Francis, PA 1996; pp. 19007–1598.

[45] Siemens G, Gasavic D. Learning and Knowledge Analytics. Journal of Educational Technology & Society. 2012;15:1–2.

[46] Siemens G, Gasevic D, Haythornthwaite C, Dawson S, Shum SB, Ferguson R, Duval E, Verbert K, Baker RS. Open Learning Analytics: an integrated & modularized platform. Proposal to design, implement and evaluate an open platform to integrate heterogeneous learning analytics techniques. [Internet]. 2011. Available from: http://classroom-aid.com/wp-content/uploads/2014/04/OpenLearningAnalytics.pdf [Accessed: 2016-05-26]

[47] Börner K. Visual analytics in support of education. In: Proceedings of the 2nd International Conference on Learning Analytics and Knowledge (LAK '12); 29 April 29 – 02 May 2012; New York, New York. p. 2–3.

[48] Ware C. Information Visualization: Perception for Design. 2nd ed. Morgan Kaufmann Interactive Technologies Series; Burlington. 2004; pp. 351–87.

[49] Murnion P, Helfert M. Academic Analytics in quality assurance using organisational analytical capabilities. In: Proceedings of the 18th UKAIS Conference on Information Systems. 2013.18-20th March 2013; Oxford, UK. P. 53-63

Chapter 4

Medical Big Data Analysis in Hospital Information System

Jing-Song Li, Yi-Fan Zhang and Yu Tian

Additional information is available at the end of the chapter

http://dx.doi.org/10.5772/63754

Abstract

The rapidly increasing medical data generated from hospital information system (HIS) signifies the era of Big Data in the healthcare domain. These data hold great value to the workflow management, patient care and treatment, scientific research, and education in the healthcare industry. However, the complex, distributed, and highly interdisciplinary nature of medical data has underscored the limitations of traditional data analysis capabilities of data accessing, storage, processing, analyzing, distributing, and sharing. New and efficient technologies are becoming necessary to obtain the wealth of information and knowledge underlying medical Big Data. This chapter discusses medical Big Data analysis in HIS, including an introduction to the fundamental concepts, related platforms and technologies of medical Big Data processing, and advanced Big Data processing technologies.

Keywords: medical Big Data analysis, hospital information system, cloud computing, data mining, Semantic Web technologies

1. Introduction

With the deepening of hospital information construction, the medical data generated from hospital information system (HIS) have been growing at an unprecedentedly rapid rate, which signifies the era of Big Data in the healthcare domain. These data hold great value to the workflow management, patient care and treatment, scientific research, and education in the healthcare industry. As a domain-specific form of Big Data, medical Big Data include features of volume, variety, velocity, validity, veracity, value, and volatility, commonly dubbed as the seven Vs of Big Data [1]. These characteristics of healthcare data, if exploited timely and appropriately, can bring enormous benefits in the form of cost savings, improved healthcare quality, and better productivity.

However, the complex, distributed, and highly interdisciplinary nature of medical data has underscored the limitations of traditional data analysis capabilities of data accessing, storage, processing, analysing, distributing, and sharing. New and efficient technologies, such as cloud computing, data mining, and Semantic Web technologies, are becoming necessary to obtain, utilize, and share the wealth of information and knowledge underlying these medical Big Data.

This chapter discusses medical Big Data analysis in HIS, including an introduction to the fundamental concepts, related platforms and technologies of medical Big Data processing (Section 2), and advanced Big Data processing technologies (Section 3, Section 4, and Section 5). In order to help readers understand more intuitively and intensively, two case studies are given to demonstrate the method and application of Big Data processing technologies (**Section 6**), including one for medical cloud platform construction for medical Big Data processing and one for semantic framework development to provide clinical decision support based on medical Big Data.

2. Medical Big Data in HIS

In the field of medical and health care, due to the diversity of the medical records, the heterogeneity of healthcare information systems and the widespread application of HIS, the capacity of medical data is constantly growing. Major data resources include: (1) life sciences data, (2) clinical data, (3) administrative data, and (4) social network data. These data resources are invaluable for disease prediction, management and control, medical research, and medical informatization construction.

Currently, there are two directions for designing Big Data processing systems, i.e., centralized computation and distributed computation. Centralized computation relies on mainframes, which are very expensive to implement. Besides, there still exists a bottleneck for scalable data processing using a single computer system; distributed computation relies on clusters of cheap commercial computers. Due to the scalability of cluster scale, the data processing ability of distributed computing systems is also scalable. Currently, Hadoop, Spark, and Storm are the most commonly used distributed Big Data processing platforms, which are all open source and free of charge.

Hadoop [2] is the core project of Apache foundation now; its development until now has already gone through many versions. Due to its open-source character, Hadoop becomes the de facto international standard for distributed computing system, and its technical ecosystem becomes larger and larger and more and more perfect, which covers all aspects of Big Data processing. The most fundamental Hadoop platform comes from the three technical articles from Google, including three parts, first the MapReduce distributed computing framework [3], second, the distributed file system (Hadoop distributed file system, HDFS) based on Google File System (GFS) [4], and third, the HBase data storage system based on Big Table [5].

Spark [6], another open-source project of the Apache foundation developed by a lab of the University of California, Berkeley, is another important distributed computing system. Spark achieves architecture improvement on the basis of Hadoop. The most essential difference between Hadoop and Spark is that Hadoop uses hard disk for saving original data, intermediate results, and final results, while Spark uses memory directly for saving these data. Thus, the computing speed of Spark could be 100 times than Hadoop in theory. However, since memory data will be missing after power failure, Spark is not suitable for processing data with long-term storage demand.

Storm [7], a free and open-source real-time distributed computing system, developed by BackType team of Twitter, is an incubated project of the Apache foundation. Storm offers real-time computation for implementing Big Data stream processing on the basis of Hadoop. Different from the above two processing platforms, Storm itself does not have the function of collecting and saving data; it uses the Internet to receive and process stream data online directly and post back analysis results directly through the network online.

Up to now, Hadoop, Spark, and Storm are the most popular and significant distributed cloud computing technologies in Big Data field. All the three systems have their own advantage for processing different types of Big Data; both Hadoop and Spark are off-line, but Hadoop is more complex, while Spark owns higher processing speed. Storm is online and available for real-time tasks. In medical industry, the data are more and have different application scenarios. We can build specific medical Big Data processing platform and develop and deploy related Big Data applications according to characters of the three different platforms while processing different types of medical Big Data with different demands.

A complete data processing workflow includes data acquisition, storage and management, analysis, and application. The technologies of each data processing step are as follows:

Big Data acquisition, as the basic step of Big Data process, aims to collect a large amount of data both in size and type by a variety of ways. To confirm data timeliness and reliability, implementing distributed platform-based high-speed and high-reliable data fetching or acquisition (extract) collection technologies are required to realize the high-speed data integration technology for data parsing, transforming and loading. In addition, data security technology is developed to ensure data consistency and security.

Big Data storage and management technology need to solve both physical and logical level issues. At the physical level, it is necessary to build reliable distributed file system, such as the HDFS, to provide highly available, fault-tolerant, configurable, efficient, and low-cost Big Data storage technology. At the logical level, it is essential to develop Big Data modelling technology to provide distributed non-relational data management and processing ability and heterogeneous data integration and organization ability.

Big Data analysis, as the core of the Big Data processing part, aims to mine the values hidden in the data. Big Data analysis follows three principles, namely processing all the data, not the random data; focusing on the mixture, not the accuracy; getting the association relationship, not the causal relationship. These principles are different from traditional data processing in data analysis requirements, direction, and technical requirements. With huge amounts of data, simply relying on a single server computing capacity does not satisfy the timeliness requirement of Big Data processing parallel processing technology. For example, MapReduce can improve the data processing speed as well as make the system facilitate high extensibility and high availability.

Big Data analysis result interpretation and presentation to users are the ultimate goal of data processing. The traditional way of data visualization, such as bar chart, histogram, scatter plot, etc., cannot meet the complexity of Big Data analysis results. Therefore, Big Data visualization technology, such as three-dimensional scatter plot, network, stream-graph, and multi-dimensional heat map, has been introduced to this field for more powerfully and visually explaining the Big Data analysis results.

3. Cloud computing and medical Big Data analysis

3.1. Overview of cloud computing

According to the national institute of standards and technology (NIST), cloud computing is a model for enabling ubiquitous, convenient, and on-demand network access to a shared pool of configurable computing resources (e.g., networks, servers, storage, applications, and services) that can be rapidly provisioned and released with minimal management effort or service provider interaction.

Cloud computing has five essential characteristics [8]:

- On-demand service: Users do not need human interaction service provider, such as a server to automatically obtain time, network storage, and other computing resources according to their needs.
- Broad network access: Users can end on any heterogeneous access to resources through the network according to standard mechanisms, such as smart phones, tablet PCs, notebooks, workstations, and thin terminals.
- Pooling resource: All computing resources (computing, networking, storage, and application resources) are 'pooled' and fully dynamically reallocated based on user needs. Different physical and virtual resources are in possession for a plurality of service users. Based on this, high level of abstraction concept, even if the user has no concept of actual physical resources or control, can also be obtained as usual computing services.
- Rapid elasticity: All computing resources can quickly and flexibly configure publishing, to provide users with an unlimited supply capacity. For users, they can ask for computing resources acquired automatically increase or decrease with distribution according to their needs.
- Managed services: Cloud computing providers need to realize the measurement and control of resources and services in order to achieve the optimal allocation of resources.

http://dx.doi.org/10.5772/63754

According to different resource categories, the cloud services are divided into three service models, i.e., Software as a Service (SaaS), Platform as a Service (PaaS), and Infrastructure as a Service (IaaS).

- SaaS: It is a new software application and delivery model. Mode applications running on a cloud infrastructure that it will be application software and services delivered over the network to the user. Applications can access through a variety of end, and the user does not manage or control the underlying software required to run their own cloud infrastructure and software maintenance.
- PaaS: It is a kind of brand new software hosting service mode, users can interface with providers and own applications hosted on the cloud infrastructure.
- IaaS: It is a new infrastructure outsourcing mode, the user can obtain basic computing resources (CPU, memory, network, etc.) according to their needs. For users, it can be deployed on the service, operation, and control of the operating system and associated application software without the need to care or realize the underlying cloud infrastructure.

To meet the different needs of users, according to the cloud infrastructure deployment pattern difference, there are basically four deployment models, namely private cloud, public cloud, community cloud, and hybrid cloud, under different requirements for the deployment of the cloud computing infrastructure.

- Private cloud: Cloud platform is designed specifically for a particular unit of service and provides the most direct and effective control of data security and quality of service. In this mode, the unit needs to invest, construct, manage, and maintain the entire cloud infrastructure, platform, and software and owns risk.
- Public cloud: Cloud service providers provide free or low-cost computing, storage, and application services. The core attributes are to a shared resource service via the Internet such as Baidu cloud and Amazon Web Service.
- Community cloud: Multiple units share using the same cloud infrastructure for they have common goals or needs. Interest, costs, and risks are assumed jointly.
- Hybrid cloud: The cloud infrastructure is a composition of two or more distinct cloud infrastructures (private, community, or public).

3.2. Technologies of cloud computing

Cloud computing is an emerging computing model, and its development depends on its own unique technology with a series of other traditional technique supports:

- Rapid deployment. Since the birth of data centre, rapid deployment is an important functional requirement. Data centre administrators and users have been in the pursuit of faster, more efficient, and more flexible deployment scheme. Cloud computing environment for rapid deployment requirements is even higher. First of all, in cloud environment, resources and application not only change in large range but also in high dynamics. The required services for users mainly adopt the on-demand deployment method. Secondly, different levels of cloud computing environment service deployment pattern are different. In addition, the deployment process supported by various forms of software system and the system structure is different; therefore the deployment tool should be able to adapt to the change of the object being deployed.

- Resource dispatching: In certain circumstances, according to certain regulations regarding the use of the resources, resource dispatching can adjust resources between different resource users. These resource users correspond to different computing tasks, and each computing tasks in the operating system corresponds to one or more processes. The emergence of virtual machine makes all computing tasks encapsulated within a virtual machine. The core technology of the virtual machine is the hypervisor. It builds an abstraction layer between the virtual machine and the underlying hardware; operating system calls to hardware interception down and provides the operating system virtual resources such as memory and CPU. At present, The Vmware ESX and Citrix XenServer can run directly on the hardware. Due to the isolation of virtual machine, it is feasible to use the virtual machine live migration technology to complete the migration of computing tasks.

- Massive data processing: With a platform of Internet, cloud computing will be more widely involved in large-scale data processing tasks. Due to the frequent operations of massive data processing, many researchers are working in support of mass data processing programming model. The world's most popular mass data processing programming model is MapReduce designed by Google. MapReduce programming model divides a task into many more granular subtasks, and these subtasks can schedule between free processing nodes making acute nodes process more tasks, which avoids slow processing speed of nodes to extend the task completion time.

- Massive message communication: A core concept of cloud computing is the resources, and software functions are released in the form of services, and it is often needed to communicate the message collaboration between different services. Therefore, reliable, safe, and high-performance communication infrastructure is vital for the success of cloud computing. Asynchronous message communication mechanism can make the internal components in each level of cloud computing and different layers decoupling and ensure high availability of cloud computing services. At present, the cloud computing environment of large-scale data communication technology is still in the stage of development.

- Massive distributed storage: Distributed storage needs storage resources to be abstract representations and unified management and be able to guarantee the safety of data read and write operations, the reliability, performance, etc. Distributed file system allows the user to access the remote server's file system like a visit to a local file system, and users can take the data stored in multiple remote servers. Mostly, distributed file system has redundant backup mechanism and the fault-tolerant mechanism to ensure the correctness of the data reading and writing. Based on distributed file system and according to the characteristics of cloud storage, cloud storage service makes the corresponding configuration and improvement.

http://dx.doi.org/10.5772/63754

3.3. Application of cloud computing in medical data analysis

With the continuous development of medical industry, expanding the scale of medical data and the increasing value, the concept of medical Big Data has become the target of many experts and scholars. In the face of the sheer scale of medical Big Data, the traditional storage architecture cannot meet the needs, and the emergence of cloud computing provides a perfect solution for the medical treatment of large data storage and call.

According to different functions, medical cloud platform is divided into five parts: cloud storage data acquisition layer, data storage layer, data mining layer, enterprise database, and application layer. Every part can form an independent child cloud. Data mining layer and application layer share using data storage layer. Medical cloud deployment is shown in **Figure 1**. The figure also illustrates the medical cloud data flow direction.

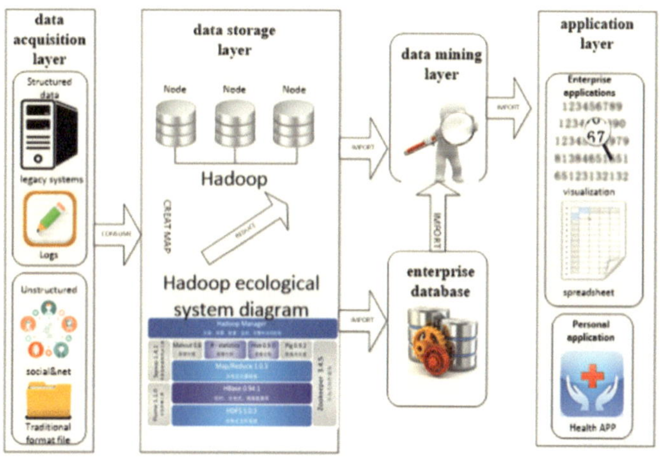

Figure 1. Medical cloud deployment.

All the parts of the medical cloud platform are specific as follows:

- Data acquisition layer: The storage format of medical large data is diverse, including the structured and unstructured or semi-structured data. So data acquisition layer needs to collect data in a variety of formats. Also, medical cloud platform and various medical systems are needed for docking and reading data from the corresponding interface. Due to the current social software and network rapid development, combining medical and social networking is the trend of the future. So it is essential to collect these data. Finally, data acquisition layer will adopt sets of different formats of data processing, in order to focus on storage.

- Data storage layer: The data storage layer stores all data of the medical cloud platform resources. Cloud storage layer data will adopt platform model for architecture and merge the data collected from data acquisition layer and block for storage.

- Data mining layer: Data mining is the most important part of medical cloud platform which complete the data mining and analysis work through the computer cluster architecture. Using the corresponding data mining algorithms, data mining layer finds knowledge from the data in data storage layer and enterprise database and store the result in data storage layer. Data mining layer can also affect application layer using its digging rules and knowledge via methods of visualization.
- Enterprise database. Medical institutions require not only convenient, large capacity of cloud storage but also high real-time and high confidentiality to local storage of data. These would require the enterprise database. Enterprise database needs interaction with data cloud storage layer and the data mining layer in data, and it will give the data to the application layer for display.
- Application layer: The application layer is mainly geared to the needs of users and displays data either original or derived through data mining.

4. Data mining and medical Big Data analysis

4.1. Overview of data mining

Cross Industry Standard Process for Data mining (CRISP-DM) is a general-purpose methodology which is industry independent, technology neutral, and the most referenced and used in practice DM methodology.

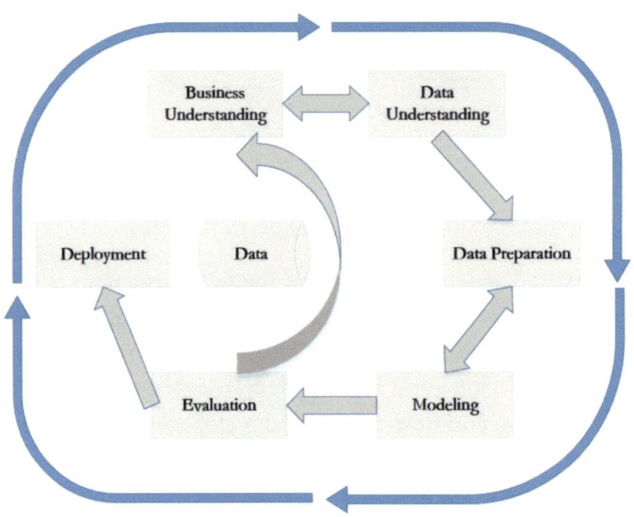

Figure 2. Phases of the original CRISP-DM reference model.

As shown in **Figure 2**, CRISP-DM proposes an iterative process flow, with non-strictly defined loops between phases and overall iterative cyclical nature of DM project itself. The outcome

http://dx.doi.org/10.5772/63754

of each phase determines which phase has to be performed next. The six phases of CRISP-DM are as follows: business understanding, data understanding, data preparation, modelling, evaluation, and deployment.

There are a few known attempts to provide a specialized DM methodology or process model for applications in the medical domain. Spečkauskienė and Lukoševičius [9] proposed a generic workflow of handling medical DM applications. However, the authors do not cover some important aspects of practical DM application, such as data understanding, data preparation, mining non-structured data, and deployment of the modelling results.

Catley et al. [10] proposed a CRISP-DM extension for mining temporal medical data of multidimensional streaming data of intensive care unit (ICU) equipment. The results of the work will benefit the researchers of ICU temporal data but not directly applicable for other medical data types or DM application goals.

Olegas Niaksu et al. [11] proposed a novel methodology, called CRISP-MED-DM, based on the CRISP-DM reference model and aimed to resolve the challenges of medical domain such as variety of data formats and representations, heterogeneous data, patient data privacy, and clinical data quality and completeness.

4.2. Technologies of data mining

There are five approaches for data mining tasks: classification, regression, clustering, association, and hybrid. Classification refers to supervised methods that determine target class value of unseen data. The process of classification is shown in **Figure 3**. In classification, the data are divided into training and test sets used for learning and validation, respectively. We have described most popular algorithms in medical data mining in **Table 1**. These algorithms are the most used in literatures and are also popular. Performance evaluation of classifiers can be measured by hold-out, random sub-sampling, cross-validation, and bootstrap. Among these, cross-validation is the most common.

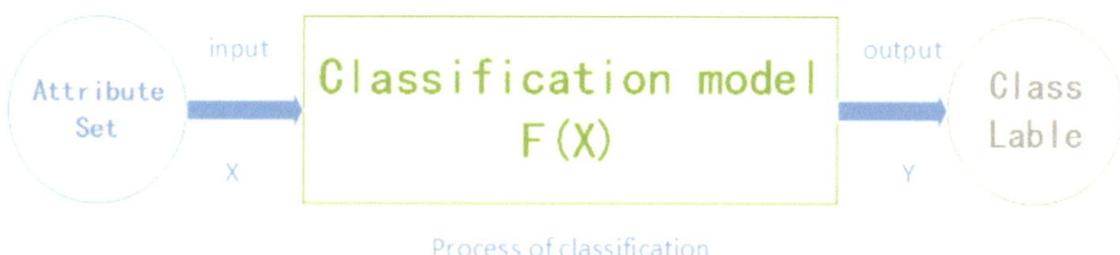

Figure 3. Process of classification.

Regression analysis is a statistical technique that estimates and predicts relations between variables. Instances of regression algorithms are simple linear, multiple linear, fuzzy, and logistic. In data mining, regression is used to predict unseen data based on continuous training data. In this approach, the behaviour of dependent variable y is explored by independent variables x.

Algorithm	Advantage	Disadvantage	Characteristic
DT	Non-parametric, interpretable, resistant to noise and replication	Separation line parallel to axis *x*, *y*, sensitive to the inconsistent data	Eager approach, greedy, recursive, partitioning, stable
ANN	Diagonal separation line, popular in the other fields, ability to complex relation, resistant to replication	Black box, parametric, sensitive to the noise and missing value, increase time by increase hidden layers	Eager approach, multi-layer network with at least one hidden layer
Rule based	Interpretable, resistant to noise and imbalance data	Separation line parallel to axis *x*, *y*	Eager approach, produce if…then rules, partitioning
SVM	Diagonal separation line, appropriate for high-dimensional data and little training data	Black box, parametric	Eager approach, mathematics based, unstable, optimization, global minimum
NB	Resistant to noise, missing value, irrelevant features	Accuracy degraded by correlated attribute, required to determine initial probability	Eager approach, statistics based, nondeterministic
KNN	Simple, flexible, arbitrary decision boundaries	Sensitive to noise and replication, parametric	Lazy approach, instance based, required similarity measurement, prediction based on local data

Table 1. Most popular classification algorithms in medical data mining.

Algorithm	Advantage	Disadvantage	Characteristic
K-means	Simple, fast, popular	Parametric, susceptible initial value, inappropriate for data different in size and density, different results in each run, sensitive to noise	Optimization problem, rototype based, partitioning problem, centre based
Hierarchical	Non-parametric, less susceptible to initial value	Time and space complexity, sensitive to noise	Graph based, prototype based, bottom-up
DBSCAN	Resistant to noise, handle arbitrary density	Time and space complexity	Density-based, non-complete, partitioning problem

Algorithm	Advantage	Disadvantage	Characteristic
	and size		
Fuzzy c-means	Same as K-means	Same as K-means	Same as K-means, determining membership of each object to the clusters

Table 2. Most popular data clustering methods.

Data clustering consists of grouping and collecting a set of objects into similar classes. In data clustering process, objects in the same cluster are similar to each other, while objects in different clusters are dissimilar. Data clustering can be seen as grouping or compression problem. Most popular data clustering methods are described in **Table 2**.

Association rule mining is a method for exploring sequential data to discover relationships between large transactional data. The result of this analysis is in the form of association rules or frequent items. In **Table 3**, most popular association algorithms are shown. Performance evaluation of discovered rules was done considering various criteria such as support and confidence.

Algorithm	Advantage	Disadvantage	Characteristic
Apriori	Popular, simple	Time and I/O complexity, reviewing entire database at each stage, searching in all variables	Using prior knowledge, iterative approach
DIC	Decrease I/O complexity	Sensitive to data homogeneity	Dynamic, retrieving lost patterns by moving forward, investigating the specified distance of transactions
DHP	Reducing the number of candidate patterns	Relation between runtime and database size, collision problem in the hash table	Using hash table
Eclat	Decreasing I/O complexity, exploring large length patterns, and discovering all sequential objects	Space complexity, inappropriate for large data	Bottom-up approach, uses lattice-theoretic
D-CLUB	Removing the empty bits, reduce time and space complexity, self-adaptive	–	Appropriate for parallel process and distributed database, dynamic, differential optimization

Table 3. Most popular association rule methods.

Among the five data mining approaches, classification is known as the most important [12]. Interpretability of model is the key factor to select the best algorithm for extracting knowledge.

It is important for the expert to understand extracted knowledge. Therefore, decision tree is the most popular method in medical data mining. SVM (Support Vector Machine) and artificial neural network are proved efficient but less popular compared with decision tree, due to the incomprehensibility.

4.3. Application of data mining in medical Big Data analysis

The electronic medical record (EMR) system has been widely used around the world and has stored lots of data till today. With the data mining technologies, we can, in turn, use the data to improve the EMR system's performance, reduce medication errors, avoid adverse drug events, forecast patient outcomes, improve clinical documentation accuracy and completeness, increase clinician adherence to clinical guidelines, and contain costs and medical researches. However, the highest functional level of the electronic health record (EHR) is process automation and clinical decision support (CDS), which are expected to enhance patient health and healthcare.

4.3.1. Data mining for better system user experience

Tao et al. developed a closed-loop control scheme of electronic medical record (EMR) based on a business intelligence (BI) system to enhance the performance of hospital information system (HIS), which provides a new idea to improve the interaction design of EMR. The ranking of drugs in EMR for certain doctor is optimized and personalized based on his/her

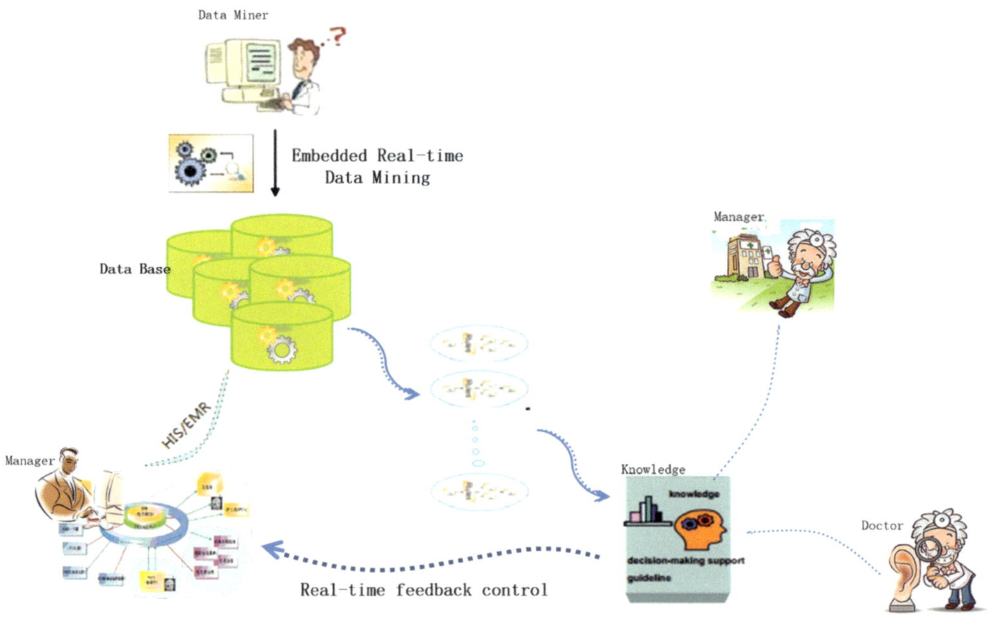

Figure 4. Closed-loop HIS.

real-time pharmacy ranking. This illustrates the important applications of a BI system to automatically control the EMR. In addition, the applicability of drug ranking is verified. The system workflow is displayed in **Figure 4**.

Using this EMR system, the ranking of drugs in the EMR is optimized with the real-time ranking of the doctor's pharmacies. With automated drug order in EMR, it realizes a personalized function for doctors, making doctors more convenient to make prescriptions compared to an irregular drug order. In addition, doctors can make orders faster with the help of personalized EMR.

4.3.2. Data mining for clinical decision support

Michael J. Donovan et al. [13] developed a predictive model for prostate cancer progression after radical prostatectomy. They collected 971 patients treated with radical prostatectomy at Memorial Sloan-Kettering Cancer Centre (MSKCC) between 1985 and 2003 for localized and locally advanced prostate cancer and for whom tissue samples were available. Although the patient number is relatively small, the dimension is high that they included clinicopathologic, morphometric, molecular data, and outcome information to implement a systemic pathology approach. The complex relationships between predictors and outcomes were modelled by support vector regression (SVR) for censored data (SVRc), which is a machine learning way rather than the conventional statistical way, to take advantage of the ability of SVR to handle high dimensional data. The SVRc algorithm [14] can be summarized to minimize the following function:

$$min\frac{1}{2}\|W\|^2+\sum_{i=1}^{n}\left(C_i\xi_i+C_i^*\xi_i^*\right)$$

given the constraints:

$$y_i-\left(W\cdot\Phi\left(x_i\right)+b\right)\leq\varepsilon_i+\xi_i$$

$$\left(W\cdot\Phi\left(x_i\right)+b\right)-y_i\leq\varepsilon_i^*+\xi_i^*$$

$$\xi_i^{(*)}\geq 0, i=1\ldots n$$

The model performance was validated by a testing data set, and it was proved to be a highly accurate tool for predicting clinical failure within 5 years after prostatectomy using the integration of clinicopathologic variables with imaging and biomarker data.

5. Semantic Web technologies and medical Big Data analysis

5.1. Overview of Semantic Web technologies

First put forward by Tim Berners-Lee, the inventor of the World Wide Web and director of the World Wide Web Consortium (W3C), the Semantic web refers to 'an extension of the current Web in which information is given a well-defined meaning, better enabling computers and people to work in cooperation' [15]. According to W3C's vision, the core mission of Semantic Web technologies is to convert the current Web, dominated by unstructured and semi-structured documents into a meaningful 'Web of data'. The ultimate goal of the Web of data is to enable computers to do more useful work and to develop systems that can support trusted interactions over the network. To support this vision, the W3C has developed a set of standards and tools to enable human readable and computer interpretable representation of the concepts, terms, and relationships within a given knowledge domain, which can be illustrated by the Semantic Web Stack. As shown in **Figure 5**, it is a layered specification of increasingly expressive languages for metadata, where each layer exploits and uses capabilities of the layers below.

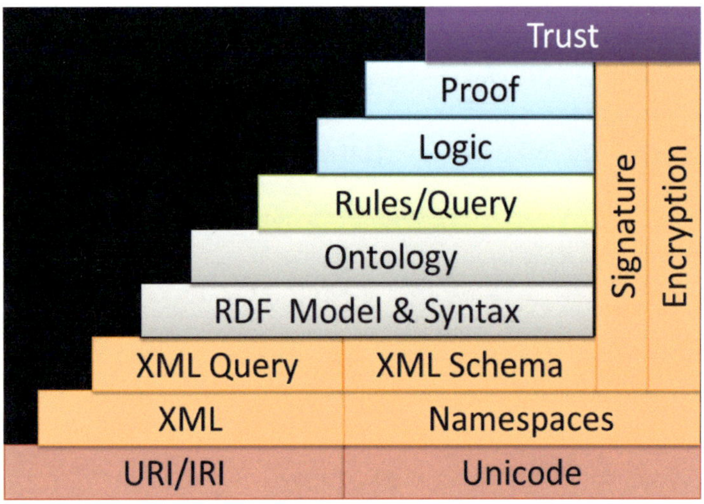

Figure 5. Semantic web stack.

All layers of the stack need to be implemented to achieve full visions of the Semantic Web. The functions and relationships of each layer can be summarized as follows:

1. Hypertext Web technologies: The well-known hypertext web technologies constitute the basic layer of the Semantic Web.

    - Internationalized resource identifier (IRI), the generalized form of the uniform resource identifier (URI), is used to uniquely identify resources on the Semantic Web with Unicode, which serves to uniformly represent and manipulate text in many languages

- Extendable mark-up language (XML) is a mark-up language that enables the creation of documents composed of structured data. XML namespaces are used for providing uniquely named elements and attributes in an XML document so that the ambiguity among more sources can be resolved to connect data together. XML schema is a description of a type of XML document, typically expressed in terms of constraints on the structure and content of documents of that type, above and beyond the basic syntactical constraints imposed by XML itself. XML query is to provide flexible query facilities to extract data from XML files.

2. Standardized Semantic Web technologies: Middle layers contain technologies standardized by W3C to enable building Semantic Web applications.

   - Resource description framework (RDF) is a framework for creating statements about Semantic Web resources in a form of 'subject-predicate-object' triples. A collection of RDF statements intrinsically represents a labelled, directed multi-graph. As such, an RDF-based data model is more suited for lightweight, flexible, and efficient knowledge representation than relational models. RDF Schema (RDFS) is intended to structure RDF resources by providing basic vocabulary for RDF.

   - Ontology is at the core of the Semantic Web Stack. It is originally defined as 'a formal, explicit specification of a shared conceptualization' [16]. By formally defining terms, relations, and constraints of commonly agreed concepts in a particular domain, ontology facilitates knowledge sharing and reuse in a declarative and computational formalism. Combined with rules and query languages, the static knowledge in the ontology can be dynamically utilized for semantic interoperation between systems.

   - Logic consists of rules that enable advanced ontology-based inferences. These rules extended the expressivity of ontology with formal rule representation languages.

3. Unrealized Semantic Web technologies: Some technologies are proposed to realize a 'safer' Semantic Web, yet most of which have not come into a standard.

   - Encryption is used to verify the reliability of data sources supporting the Semantic Web, typically using digital signature of RDF statements.

   - Proof has been conceived to allow the explanation of given answers generated by automated agents. This will require the translation of Semantic Web reasoning mechanisms into some unifying proof representation language.

   - Trust is supported by verifying that the premises come from trusted source and by relying on formal logic during deriving new information.

5.2. Semantic Web modelling languages and application framework

The OWL Web Ontology Language (OWL) is a W3C recommended mark-up language for representing ontologies [17]. Compared with XML, RDF, and RDFS, OWL has more facilities for expressing semantics and thus goes beyond these languages in its ability to represent machine interpretable content on the Web. OWL is built upon the description logic (DL), which is a family of formal knowledge representation languages used in artificial intelligence to describe and reason about the relevant concepts of an application domain. Major constructs of OWL include individuals, classes, properties, and operations. The W3C-endorsed OWL specification includes three variants of OWL, with different levels of expressiveness. These are OWL Lite, OWL DL, and OWL Full, ordered by increasing expressiveness. Each of these sublanguages is a syntactic extension of its simpler predecessor. They are designed for use by different communities of implementers and users with varying requirements for knowledge representation.

SWRL, the Semantic Web Rule Language, is a W3C recommended encoding language for representing logic rules in the Semantic Web. It extends the expressivity of OWL ontologies with the Unary/Binary Datalog RuleML sublanguages of the rule markup language. SWRL rules are represented as 'antecedent→consequent', indicating a derivation relationship from the antecedent conditions to the consequent conditions. Both the antecedent and consequent consist of zero or more atoms, written as '$a_1 \wedge a_2 \ldots \wedge a_n$'. Atoms can be of the form C(x) or P(x,y) where C is an OWL description, P is an OWL property, and x,y are either variables, OWL individuals, or OWL data values. Variables are prefixed with a question mark (e.g., ?x). Besides these basic atoms, SWRL provides modular, extensible, and reusable built-in atoms (identified using the http://www.w3.org/2003/11/swrlb namespace) as the flexible and robust infrastructure for specialized logical operations, such as swrlb:equal, swrlb:lessThan, and swrlb:greaterThanOrEqual for numeric comparisons; swrlb:add, swrlb:subtract, and swrlb:multiply for math operations; and swrlb:stringConcat, swrlb:uppercase, and swrlb:replace for string operations. A complete specification of SWRL built-in atoms can be found in [18].

Apache Jena (or Jena in short) is a free and open-source Java framework for building Semantic Web and linked data applications [19]. The framework is composed of different APIs (Application Programming Interface, API) interacting together to process RDF data. Providing various APIs for the development of inference engines and storage models, Jena is widely used in the development of systems or tools related with Web ontology management.

Jena has the following main features:

1. RDF API: Interacting with the core API, users can create and read resource description framework (RDF) graphs. The API can be used to serialize triples using popular formats such as RDF/XML and Turtle.

2. ARQ (SPARQL): It's a SPARQL 1.1 compliant engine which can be used to query RDF data. ARQ supports remote-federated queries and free text search.

3. TDB: It has a native high performance triple store and can be used to persist data. TDB supports the full range of Jena APIs.

4. Fuseki: It can be used to expose the triples as a SPARQL end-point accessible over HTTP. Fuseki provides REST-style interaction with RDF data.

5. Ontology API. It can be used to work with models, RDFS, and the Web Ontology Language (OWL) to add extra semantics to RDF data.

http://dx.doi.org/10.5772/63754

6. Inference API: It can be used to reason over the data to expand and check the content of the triple store. Users can use it to configure their own inference rules or use the built-in OWL and RDFS reasoners.

The interaction between the different APIs is shown in **Figure 6**.

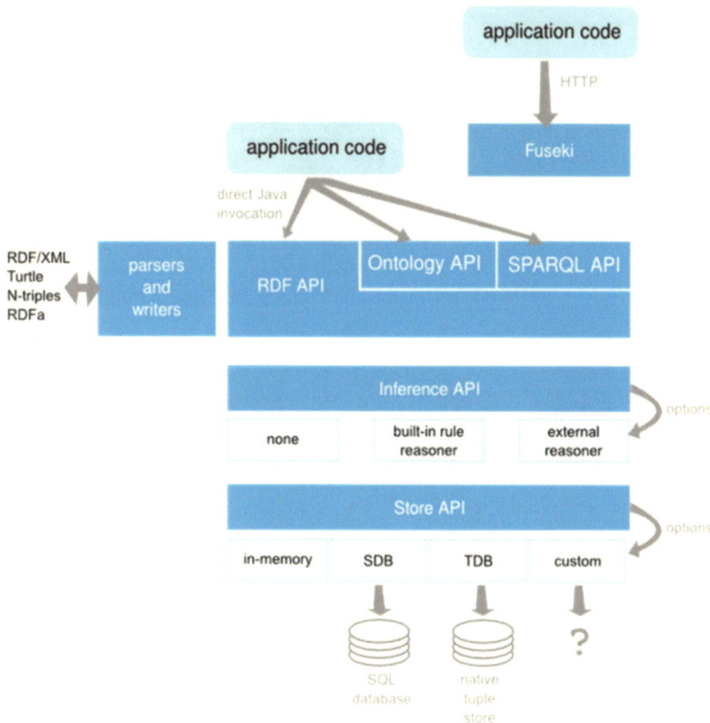

Figure 6. Interaction between the different APIs of Jena.

5.3. The applications of Semantic technology in the analysis of medical Big Data

The volume, velocity, and variety of medical data, which is being generated exponentially from biomedical research and electronic patient records, require special techniques and technologies [20]. Semantic Web technologies are meant to deal with these issues.

The Semantic Web is a collaborative movement, which promoted standard for the annotation and integration of data. Its aim is to convert the current web, dominated by unstructured and semi-structured documents, into a web of data, by encouraging the inclusion of semantic content in data accessible through the Internet.

The development of ontology on the basis of Semantic Web standards can be seen as a promising approach for a semantic-based integration of medical information. Many resources have ontology support, due to its consistency and expressivity. Important ontologies include UMLS [21], GO [22], UniProt [23], and so on.

The following diagram in **Figure 7** is an example showing the application of ontology in the big picture of Big Data analysis [20].

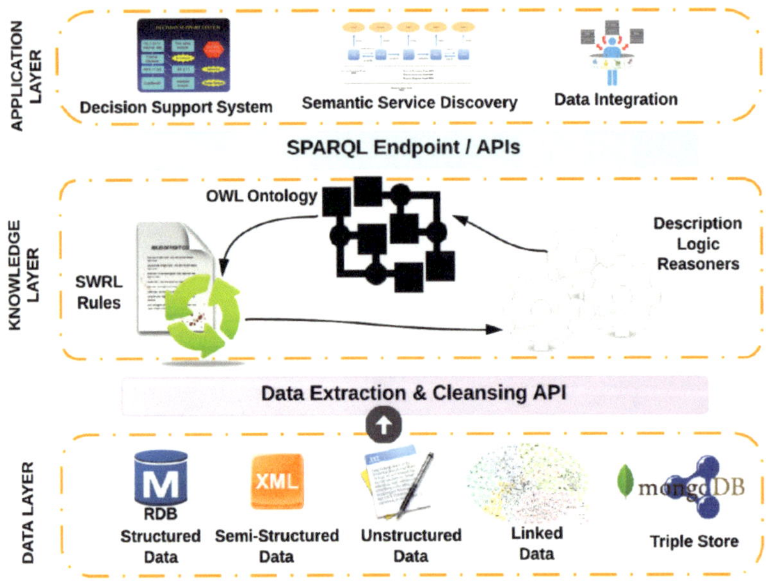

Figure 7. Ontology and rules in the big picture of Big Data analysis.

The picture includes three layers: the data layer, knowledge layer, and the application layer. The data layer consists of a wide variety of heterogeneous and complex data including structured, semi-structured, and unstructured. In the knowledge layer, ontology can be used to access Big Data, which can be processed and analysed by the ontology, rules, and reasoners to derive inferences and obtain new knowledge from it. Then in the application layer, there are several applications that can use the new knowledge such as decision support, semantic service discovery, and data integration.

6. Two case studies of medical Big Data analysis in HIS

6.1. Medical cloud platform construction for medical Big Data processing

The medical cloud platform for Big Data processing is mainly divided into three levels wherein the first level achieves a hospital private cloud, which serves as the basis of the three-tier application model. It's the IaaS service model that achieves the infrastructure of a medical cloud and also reflects the core concept of 'maximization of resource utilization' in cloud computing. The second level achieves the medical community cloud, which is an upgrade based on the first level and achieves a medical cloud service. It is software-as-a-service (SaaS) service model that reflects the core concept of 'on-demand services' in cloud computing. The third level achieves the applications of medical Big Data. It builds a medical Big Data processing system based on a distributed computing platform named Hadoop.

6.1.1. Hospital private cloud based on virtualization technology

The overall architecture of hospital private cloud is shown in **Figure 8**. It is based on the concept of 'pool', and five standard IT resource pools (virtual computing pool, virtual storage pool, virtual network pool, virtual desktop pool, and virtual security pool) are built by highly integrating and fully making use of hospital information resources using virtualization, loading balancing, and high-availability technology. Besides, the dynamic data centre based on cloud computing technology and hospital information cloud service platform consisting of five business function clouds (production cloud, testing cloud, desktop cloud, security cloud, and disaster backup cloud) are also built in the hospital private cloud. All of the above realize unified deployment of systems, assignment on demand of resources, and security sharing of data in the platform, causing the improvement of overall utilization of IT resource and the full use of the performance of information systems, which comprehensively solve the problems existing in the traditional hospital IT structure.

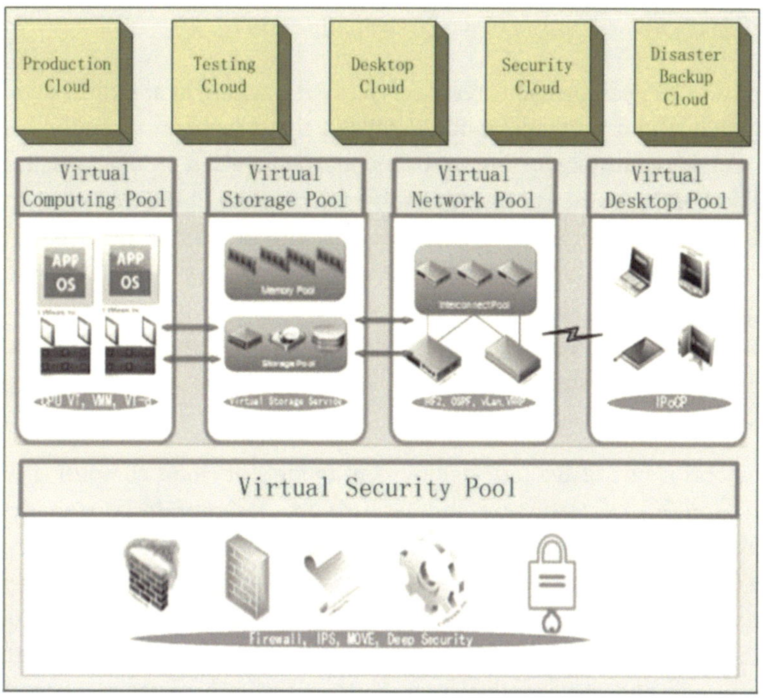

Figure 8. The overall architecture of hospital private cloud.

In five virtual IT resource pools, virtual computing pool realizes the abstract of physical hardware resources by multiple types of virtualization technologies, making the computing resources to be assigned, dispatched, and managed; the role of virtual storage pool is mainly for storage integration; virtual network pool uses network virtualization technology to solve the problems of the interaction of data from the clinical data centre in the medical information system, the real-time backup of medical, the transfer of virtual machine of medical information system, and other problems with large network flows; virtual desktop pool provides desktop system containing various packaged hospital information system application software; and virtual security pool divides the physical firewall into several independent logical firewall with different defence and security rules by virtualization division of the firewall device, making it easier to manage the firewall device and improve the utilization of the firewall device.

In the five business function clouds, production cloud is designed to maintain the hospital daily medical business under normal circumstances; testing cloud is designed for debugging the hospital's newly developed business systems; desktop cloud is designed to be used to provide virtual desktop delivery containing hospital information system applications; disaster backup cloud is designed for the backup of production cloud and providing the continuity of medical business under abnormal circumstances; and security cloud is designed for providing security services and user authority management.

6.1.2. Medical cloud services based on medical community cloud

Medical cloud services can provide access services everywhere in any time, regardless of the system's installation and implementation details of these services; secondly, medical cloud services can remain online forever. For the occasional unexpected problems, maintenance staff of medical cloud background can find and solve the problem at the first time, ensuring high availability and reliability of medical cloud services, providing normal medical information services; moreover, medical cloud service also supports a very large user base. By 'multi-tenancy' mode, a medical cloud platform provides tenancies of medical cloud services to multiple grassroots medical institutions. The platform can withstand the pressure of the mass of medical information system applications and data access, supporting large user base accessing the medical cloud services.

Community cloud is one of the four deployment models of cloud computing which means that cloud computing infrastructure and services are designed to be provided to certain organizations whose participants have issues of common concern. It can be owned and managed by one or more organizations and only provide relevant cloud services among the organizations. The medical community cloud is an specialization of community cloud in medicine, whose structure is shown in **Figure 9**. Its purpose is to provide ubiquitous medical information systems and services. It is an upgrade on the basis of hospital private cloud that provides major medical institutions' medical information systems as services to grassroots medical institutions by using high-speed private network. The maintenance and management of cloud infrastructure and the deployment, maintenance, and design of medical information systems are all completed by major medical institutions at the background of cloud platform, making grassroots medical institutions invest in hospital informatization at zero cost.

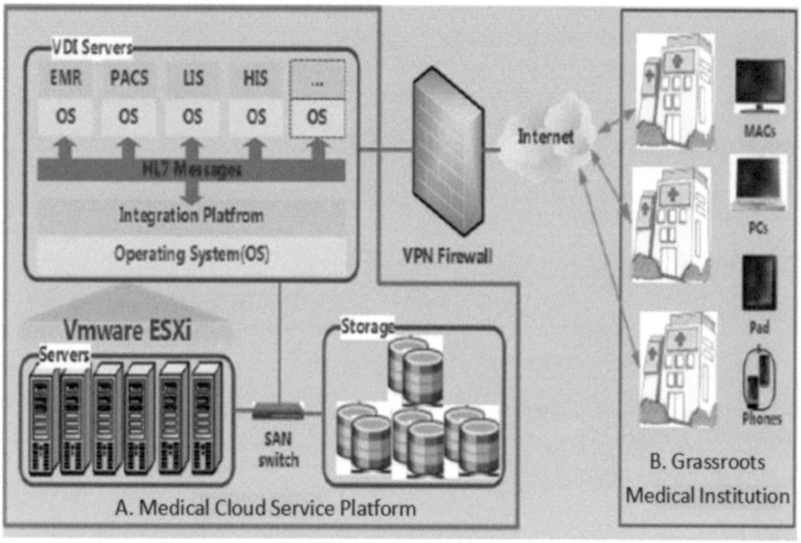

Figure 9. The structure of medical community cloud.

6.1.3. Medical Big Data systems based on distributed computing technology

An overall architecture of a medical Big Data processing system based on Hadoop is shown in **Figure 10**. The system consists of three components: (1) Big Data collection module, (2) Big Data storage management module, and (3) Big Data analysis module. The three modules respectively correspond to three processes used in solving medical Big Data processing problems: Big Data collection, Big Data storage and management, and Big Data analysis. The Big Data collection module firstly develops Extract-Transform-Load (ETL) module based on Sqoop in order to transfer structured data from relational databases to Hadoop platform and then develops transmission function of semi-structured data and unstructured data based on Hadoop Common; the Big Data storage and management module firstly realizes the physical storage of Big Data base on HDFS and then achieves logical management and high-speed access of Big Data based on Hive; and the Big Data analysis module develops Big Data recommendation engine based on Mahout. In the application of Big Data, the system provides relatively reliable personalized recommendation to the users of medical information system by its recommendation system module and a distributed collaborative filtering algorithm which reveals the collective wisdom of the medical Big Data, in order to improve the daily work efficiency. Meanwhile, to solve the limitation that Hadoop cannot achieve ad hoc query and interactive system design, the HL7 interface between recommendation system and hospital information system is developed. The interface can transfer the results into standard HL7 message in real time, realizing real-time interaction with the hospital information system. Hospital information systems, three modules of medical Big Data processing system, recommendation systems, and its HL7 interface constitute a medical Big Data closed loop of 'generation -collection-storage-analysis–feedback'.

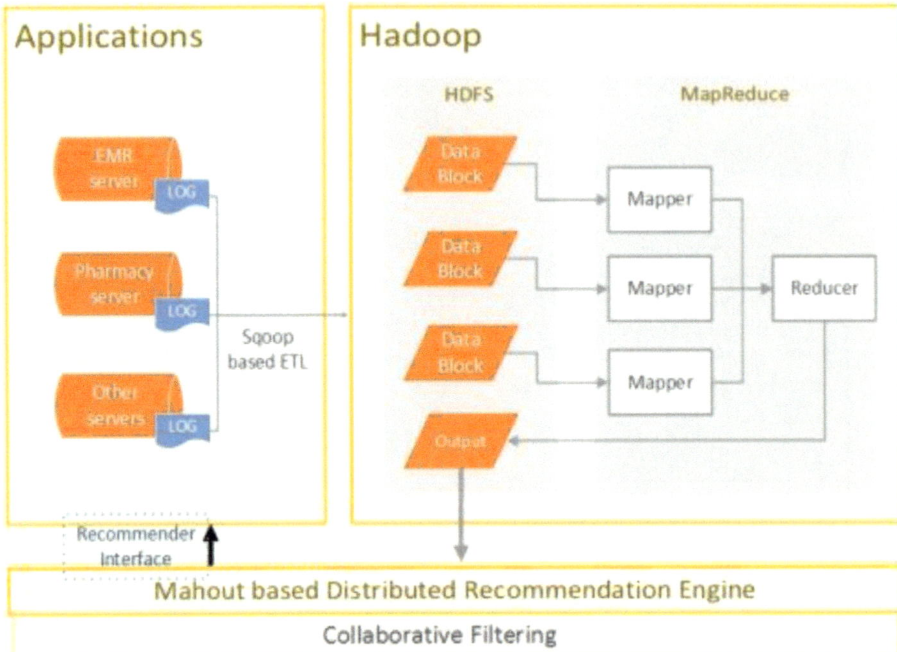

Figure 10. Overall architecture of the medical Big Data processing system.

Because the three modules of the architecture are designed in the environment based on Hadoop-distributed computing, and Hadoop cluster can provide MapReduce (distributed computing) and HDFS (distributed storage), both of which are needed for the system, the system can process medical Big Data in reasonable time. Compared to the non-distributed architecture, this architecture has a huge advantage in all the three aspects: the performance in the collection, storage, and analysis of medical Big Data.

6.2. Semantic framework development to provide clinical decision support based on medical Big Data

A clinical decision support system (CDSS) is a computer-based information system developed specifically for clinical decision-making, in which the characteristics of an individual patient are matched to a computerized clinical knowledge base, and patient-specific assessments or recommendations are then presented to the clinician or the patient for a decision [24]. A large body of evidence suggests that CDSSs can be helpful in improving clinical practice. However, to this day, CDSSs have not found wide use outside of a handful of mostly academic medical centres, and their impact on patient outcome is marginal. A major impediment to their wide adoption is the lack of standard knowledge representation formalisms and lack of efficient technologies to process medical Big Data [25]. As the knowledge used by CDSSs is typically derived from standard clinical pathways (or care plans, CPs), this section presents a CP-related case study that successfully implements the Semantic Web framework in solving the above-mentioned deficiency [26]. It proposed a data-driven clinical decision support method to improve CP practicality by applying semantic analysis and reasoning to clinical data in HIS. In addition to the standard general CP orders, detailed locally customized CP orders and mined CP orders from local treatment protocols were provided to efficiently compose hospital-specific CPs, which is beneficial for improving the practicality of CPs and contributing to improve patient-centred care quality.

6.2.1. Model construction

The study used Protégé [27] as the ontology editor tool, OWL as the ontology representation language, and Jena Semantic Web framework as the integrated platform for semantic transforming and reasoning. Global ontology containing standard CP terms and associated relationships were constructed based on the CP specifications published by the Ministry of Health of China. Semantic mapping were created to realize the semantic mapping from standard CP terms to practical clinical data represented by local ontologies, which were built based on vocabulary databases in HIS.

Four super classes, 84 subclasses, and 98 individuals were created in the final CP ontology. As depicted in **Figure 11**, SeptumDeviationCP is an individual of the CP ontology to represent the deviated nasal septum CP. Three order events of the CP are listed with their related order terms and execution dates. Every order term is assigned a value of the property hasHZTerm. The order term 'AntisepticDrug', which is a subclass of Injection, has multiple values assigned for the property hasDrugHZTerm. Standard CP orders from the CP ontology are listed according to their execution date.

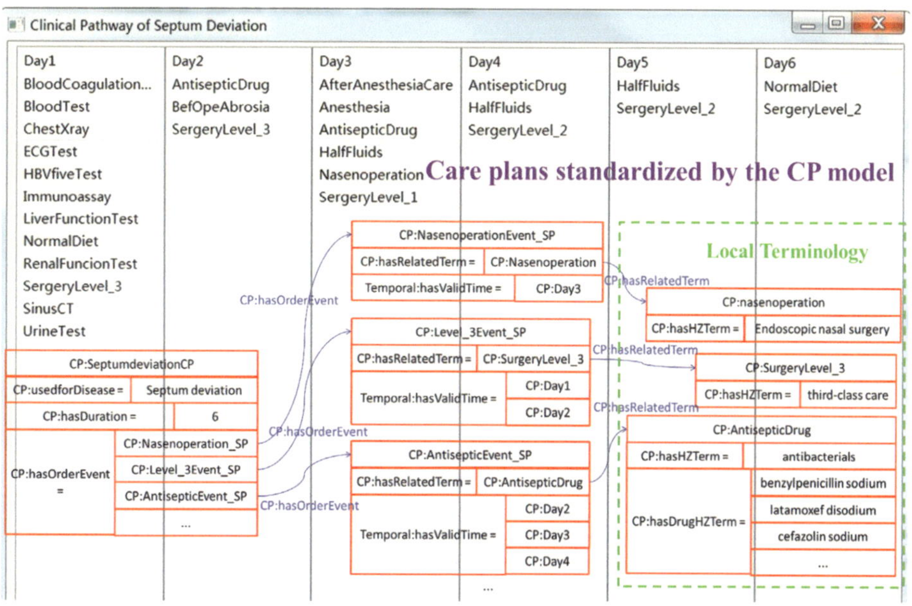

Figure 11. Care plans standardized by the CP model.

6.2.2. Semantic transformation

Semantic transformation of non-semantic relational data modelled into unified semantic data model (RDF format) solves the problem of data heterogeinity and realizes semantic level data integration; it is the foundational process of semantic reasoning and other advanced Semantic Web applications for the meaningful use of medical big data. In this study, Class OrderFact, a super class, is introduced to represent the order data. Each order record acquired by structured query language (SQL) from the relational data model is transformed to an individual of class OrderFact. Fields of order records correspond to the properties of individuals. The transformed data can be accessed and shared using the SPARQL Semantic Web query language [28]. A statistical analysis on the repetition rate of historical clinical procedures was further conducted to derive the similarity of patient treatment.

A total of 224 individuals of class patient and 11,473 individuals of class OrderFact are imported. As shown in **Figure 12**, each individual of class OrderFact includes the following nine properties: hasPatientData, hasOrderType, hasOrderCode, hasOrderName, hasRepeatIndication, hasStartDate, hasStopDate, hasExecuteDay, and hasCPFlag. In addition, two self-defined properties, hasExecuteDay and hasCPFlag, were inserted.

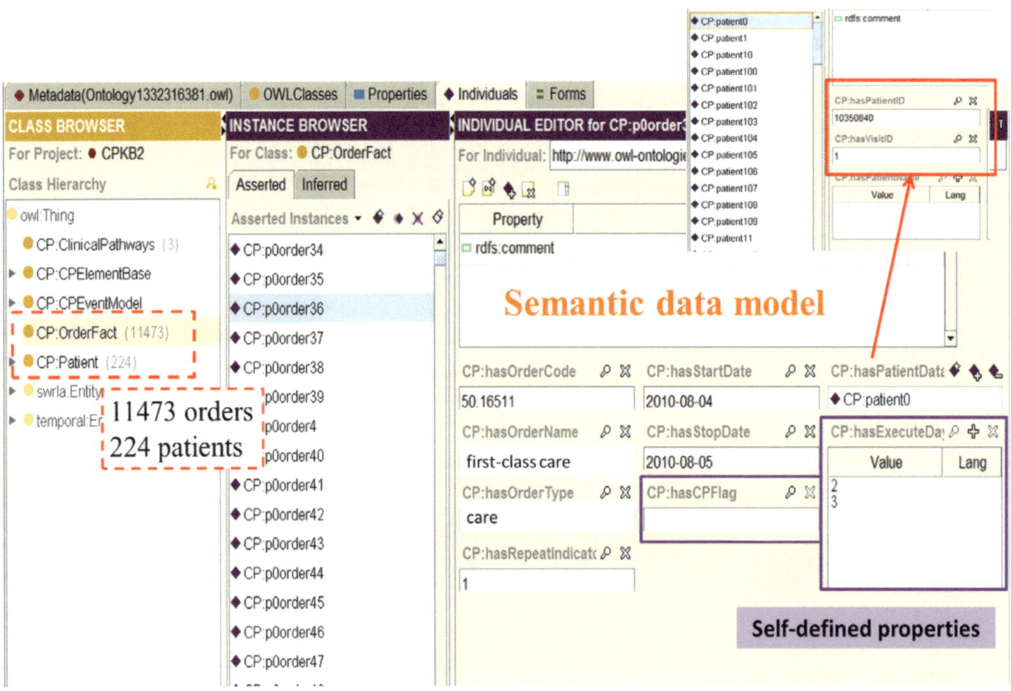

Figure 12. Semantic data model after semantic transformation.

The semantic property hasExecuteDay represents the relative execution day of each order, which is used in long-term order processing aimed at distinguishing long-time orders whose validity holds for multiple hospital days, from temporary orders whose validity holds only at a specific hospital day. This process is important to avoid possible omissions in traditional statistical methods that simply count order records in the raw data tables. The results of long-term order processing are shown in **Figure 13**. The resulting differences in treatment procedures are becoming significant since the third day. For example, detailed orders such as 'first-class care', 'second-class care', and 'third-class care' are being added to the original general nursing orders. In practice, nursing orders, diet orders, and injection orders are typically recorded as long-term orders. Therefore, long-term order processing is necessary to keep a complete track of patient longitudinal medical records.

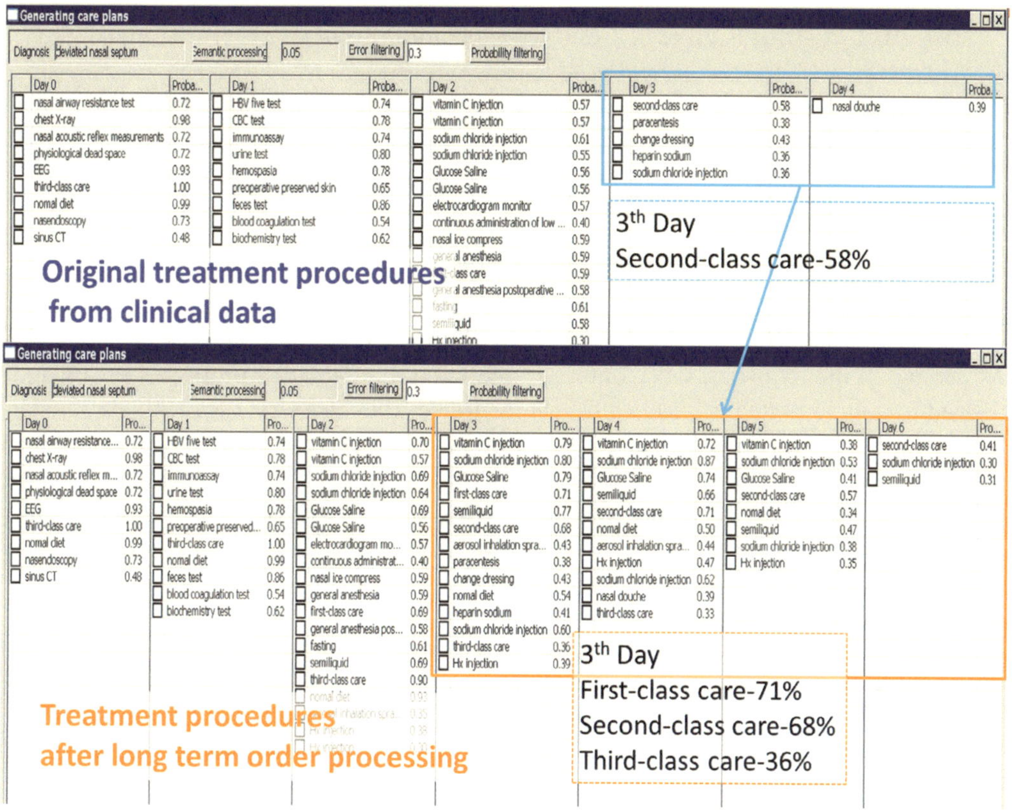

Figure 13. Results of long-term order processing.

6.2.3. A semantic reasoning

The occurrence of incorrect order records is inevitable. These incorrect order records can be categorized into two types: (1) random errors resulting from recording mistakes; these errors could be eliminated by filtering out the clinical procedures with probability less than the predetermined minimum. In addition, orders with small probability are specially given to a small number of patients, while not common to other patients. After consulting relevant domain experts, this study used 5% as the default minimum to filter out incorrect orders. A total of

2370 erroneous orders were successfully detected and removed; (2) incorrect data recorded during actual medical procedures, these errors could be eliminated by semantic reasoning. For example, in cases where equivalent long-term and temporary orders co-exist, the semantic rule Rule 1 (**Figure 14**) has been proposed to avoid repetitive ordering: ?order1 and ?order2 are instances of OrderFact, assigned with the same patient (?patient), valid execution time (?day), and title (?name). However, ?order1 is long term, while ?order2 is temporary. After semantic reasoning, the redundant execution time of ?order1 is removed.

```
Rule1:
@prefix CP: <http://www.owl-ontologies.com/Ontology1332316381.owl#>.
[ErrorData: (?order1 CP:hasPatientData ?patient)
(?order2 CP:hasPatientData ?patient)(?order1 CP:hasExecuteDay ?day)
(?order2 CP:hasExecute-Day ?day)(?order1 CP:hasOrderName ?name)
(?order2 CP:hasOrderName ?name)(?order1 CP:hasRepeatIndicator "1")
(?order2 CP:hasRepeatIndicator "0")
-> remove(2)]
```

Figure 14. Rule 1.

As defined in the following OWL ontology definition, the semantic property hasCPFlag is defined to compare actual clinical workflow identified from historical data with the standardized treatment procedures defined by the CP model. A property value of '1' signifies a direct correspondence between the data order and a CP order, while '2' signifies that the data order provides more details of the CP order. Rule 2 (**Figure 15**) specifies the criteria for determining this property value by comparing the order name (?name) of a data order with the term assigned to hasHZTerm.

```
Rule2:
[BasicCPOrder:(?order CP:hasOrderName ?name)
(CP:SeptumdeviationCP CP:hasOrderEvent ?order_event)
(?order_event CP:hasRelatedTerm ?order_term)
(?order_term CP:hasHZTerm ?name)
-> (?order CP:hasCPFlag 1)]
```

Figure 15. Rule 2.

A common problem of implementing standard CPs in a local health care setting is the lack of details such as prescription dose and frequency, which can be mined from local data records. In Rule 3 (**Figure 16**), orders mined from data records which provide such supplemental information of standard CP orders are inferred with hasCPFlag value '2', meaning 'deduced pathway orders'.

http://dx.doi.org/10.5772/63754

```
Rule3:
[DrugCPOrder:(?order CP:hasOrderName ?name)
(CP:SeptumdeviationCP CP:hasOrderEvent ?order_event)
(?order_event CP:hasRelatedTerm ?order_term)
(?order_term CP:hasDrugHZTerm ?name)
-> (?order CP:hasCPFlag 2)]
```

Figure 16. Rule 3.

The reasoning results of executing the Jena rule Rule 1 are shown in **Figure 17**. Take the orders in the second day as an example. There exist reduplicate injection orders for injections such as vitamin C (70 and 57%), sodium chloride (69 and 64%), and glucose saline (69 and 54%) in preoperative treatment procedures. After reasoning, recurrences are removed. Long-term order processing using Rule 1 makes the recorded treatment process more consistent with clinical practice, improving data quality for further analysis.

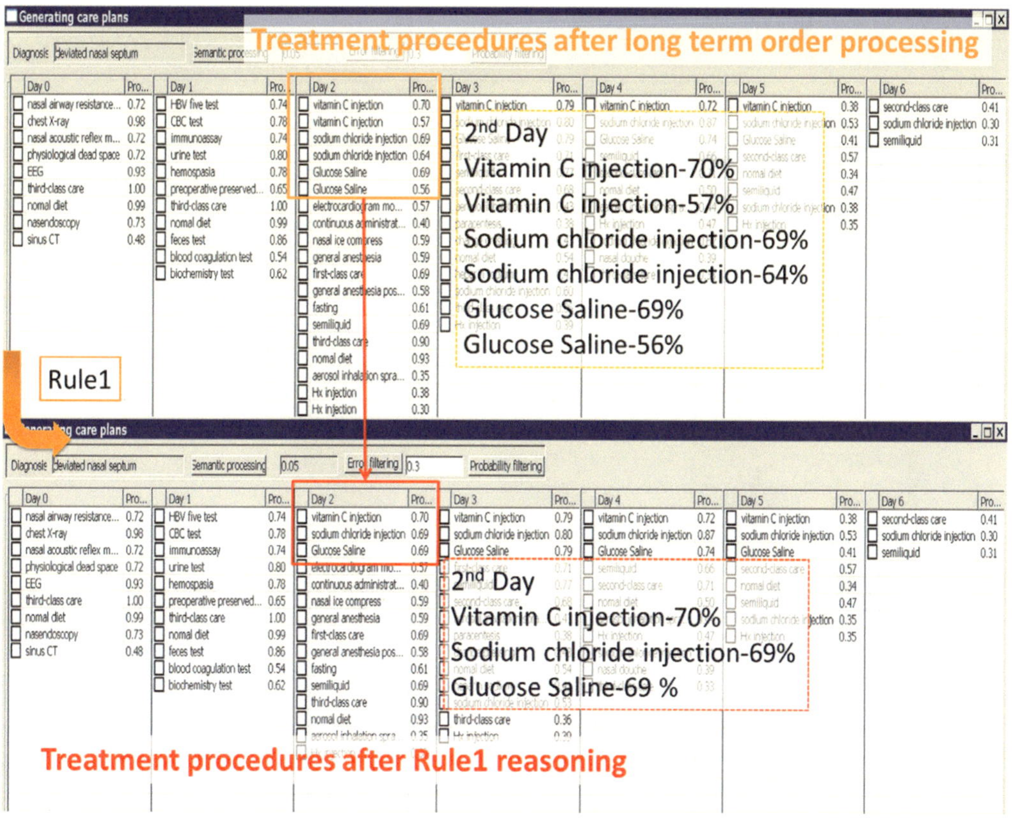

Figure 17. Reasoning results of executing Rule 1.

Figure 18. Reasoning results of executing Rule 2 and Rule 3.

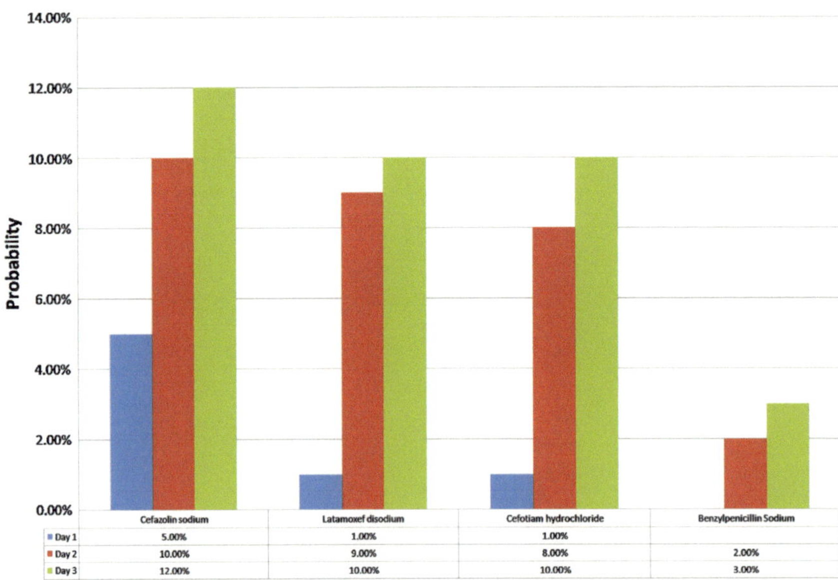

Figure 19. A detailed description of the pathway order "antibacterial."

http://dx.doi.org/10.5772/63754

As depicted in **Figure 18**, different item backgrounds in each child table illustrate the different reasoning results after executing Rule 2 and Rule 3. Orders with a blue background are pathway orders, while orders with a red background or an asterisk are deduced pathway orders, which specify and detail the general knowledge of pathway orders in the CP model. The results show that cefazolin sodium, latamoxef disodium, cefotiam hydrochloride, and benzyl penicillin sodium are common antibacterial drugs for patients with a deviated nasal septum. **Figure 19** presents the probabilities of four detailed antibacterial drugs being prescribed from hospital day one to day three.

Probability of pathway orders refers to the probability of pathway orders that appear in historical data, while percentage of pathway orders is defined as the percentage of pathway orders with some probability in all pathway orders. After calculating the percentage of each pathway order with different probabilities, the practical statistical data are plotted. The plot results are shown in **Figure 20**.

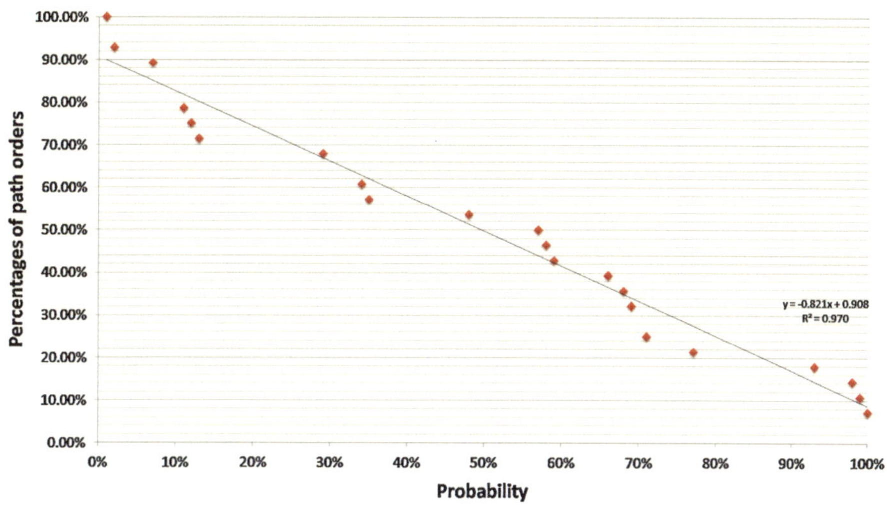

Figure 20. Percentage of each pathway order with different probabilities.

By conducting curve fitting, the percentage of pathway orders and the corresponding probability demonstrates a linear relationship, as given in the following equation, where y stands for the percentage of pathway orders, x stands for the probability, respectively.

$$\mathrm{y} = -0.821x + 0.908;\ \mathrm{k} = 0.821;\ y0 = 0.908$$

This study combines traditional statistical methods with advanced semantic technologies to improve the practicability of CPs, which enable timely clinical decision support for healthcare practitioners in balancing evidence-based care with clinical practice, with a final goal of improving healthcare quality, efficiency, and patient satisfaction.

Author details

Jing-Song Li*, Yi-Fan Zhang and Yu Tian

*Address all correspondence to: ljs@zju.edu.cn

Zhejiang University, Hangzhou, China

References

[1] Ali-Ud-Din Khan M, Uddin MF, Gupta N, editors. Seven V's of big data understanding big data to extract value. In: Conference of the American Society for Engineering Education (ASEE Zone 1); 2014. IEEE.

[2] White T. Hadoop: the definitive guide. O'reilly Media Inc Gravenstein Highway North. 2010;215(11):1–4.

[3] Dean J, Ghemawat S, Usenix. MapReduce: simplified data processing on large clusters. Berkeley: Usenix Assoc; 2004. 137–49 p.

[4] Ghemawat S, Gobioff H, Leung S-T. The google file system. SIGOPS Operating Systems Review. 2003;37(5):29–43.

[5] Chang F, Dean J, Ghemawat S, et al. Bigtable: A distributed storage system for structured data[J]. ACM Transactions on Computer Systems (TOCS), 2008, 26(2): 4.

[6] Zaharia M, Chowdhury M, Franklin MJ, Shenker S, Stoica I. Spark: cluster computing with working sets. Book of Extremes. 2010;15(1):1765–73.

[7] Iqbal MH, Soomro TR. Big data analysis: apache storm perspective. International Journal of Computer Trends & Technology. 2015;19(1):9–14.

[8] Stieninger M, Nedbal D. Characteristics of cloud computing in the business context: a systematic literature review. Global Journal of Flexible Systems Management. 2014;15(1):59–68.

[9] Špečkauskienė V, Lukoševičius A. A data mining methodology with preprocessing steps. Information Technology and Control. 2015;38(4)319–323.

[10] Catley C, Smith K, McGregor C, et al. Extending CRISP-DM to incorporate temporal data mining of multidimensional medical data streams: A neonatal intensive care unit case study[C]//Computer-Based Medical Systems, 2009. CBMS 2009. 22nd IEEE International Symposium on. IEEE, 2009: 1–5.

[11] Niaksu O. CRISP data mining methodology extension for medical domain. Baltic Journal of Modern Computing. 2015;3(2):92.

[12] Esfandiari N, Babavalian MR, Moghadam A-ME, Tabar VK. Knowledge discovery in medicine: current issue and future trend. Expert Systems with Applications. 2014;41(9): 4434–63.

[13] Donovan MJ, Hamann S, Clayton M, Khan FM, Sapir M, Bayer-Zubek V, et al. Systems pathology approach for the prediction of prostate cancer progression after radical prostatectomy. Journal of Clinical Oncology Official Journal of the American Society of Clinical Oncology. 2008;26(24):3923–9.

[14] Khan F M, Zubek V B. Support vector regression for censored data (SVRc): a novel tool for survival analysis[C]//Data Mining, 2008. ICDM'08. Eighth IEEE International Conference on Data Mining. IEEE, 2008: 863–868. Conference Location : Pisa.

[15] Berners-Lee T, Hendler J, Lassila O. The semantic web. Scientific American. 2001;284(5): 28–37.

[16] Studer R, Benjamins VR, Fensel D. Knowledge engineering: principles and methods. Data & Knowledge Engineering. 1998;25(1):161–97.

[17] Mcguiness DL, Harmelen FV, Mcguiness DL. Owl web ontology language overview: W3C recommendation (10 February 2004). W3c Recommendation. 2004;63(45):990–6.

[18] Horrocks I, Patel-Schneider P F, Boley H, et al. SWRL: A semantic web rule language combining OWL and RuleML[J]. W3C Member submission, 2004, 21: 79.

[19] Mcbride B. Jena: a semantic web toolkit. Internet Computing IEEE. 2002;6(6):55–9.

[20] Shah T, Rabhi F, Ray P. Investigating an ontology-based approach for big data analysis of inter-dependent medical and oral health conditions. Cluster Computing. 2015 Mar; 18(1):351–67. PubMed PMID: WOS:000350395500031. English.

[21] Bodenreider O. The unified medical language system (UMLS): integrating biomedical terminology. Nucleic Acids Research. 2004;32(suppl 1):D267–70.

[22] Ashburner M, Ball CA, Blake JA, Botstein D, Butler H, Cherry JM, et al. Gene ontology: tool for the unification of biology. Nature Genetics. 2000;25(1):25–9.

[23] Consortium U P. Reorganizing the protein space at the Universal Protein Resource (UniProt).[J]. Nucleic Acids Research, 2011, 1–5 doi:10.1093/nar/gkr981.

[24] Sim I, Gorman P, Greenes RA, Haynes RB, Kaplan B, Lehmann H, et al. Clinical decision support systems for the practice of evidence-based medicine. Journal of the American Medical Informatics Association. 2001;8(6):527–34.

[25] Jaspers MW, Smeulers M, Vermeulen H, Peute LW. Effects of clinical decision-support systems on practitioner performance and patient outcomes: a synthesis of high-quality systematic review findings. Journal of the American Medical Informatics Association. 2011;18(3):327–34.

[26] Wang HQ, Zhou TS, Tian LL, Qian YM, Li JS. Creating hospital-specific customized clinical pathways by applying semantic reasoning to clinical data. Journal of Biomedical Informatics. 2014;52:354–63.

[27] Green M, Björk J, Forberg J, Ekelund U, Edenbrandt L, Ohlsson M. Comparison between neural networks and multiple logistic regression to predict acute coronary syndrome in the emergency room. Artificial Intelligence in Medicine. 2006;38(3):305–18.

[28] Frykberg ER. Medical management of disasters and mass casualties from terrorist bombings: how can we cope? Journal of Trauma-Injury Infection and Critical Care. 2002 Aug;53(2):201–12. PubMed PMID: WOS:000177541000001. English.

Chapter 5

PESSCARA: An Example Infrastructure for Big Data Research

Panagiotis Korfiatis and Bradley Erickson

Additional information is available at the end of the chapter

http://dx.doi.org/10.5772/63815

Abstract

Big data requires a flexible system for data management and curation which has to be intuitive, and it should also be able to execute non-linear analysis pipelines suitable to handle with the nature of big data. This is certainly true for medical images where the amount of data grows exponentially every year and the nature of images rapidly changes with technological advances and rapid genomic advances. In this chapter, we describe a system that provides flexible management for medical images plus a wide array of associated metadata, including clinical data, genomic data, and clinical trial information. The system consists of open-source Content Management System (CMS) that has a highly configurable workflow; has a single interface that can store, manage, enable curation, and retrieve imaging-based studies; and can handle the requirement for data auditing and project management. Furthermore, the system can be extended to interact with all the modern big data analysis technologies.

Keywords: big data, data analysis, content management system, curation, 3D imaging, workflows, REST API

1. Introduction

Big data is the term applied for data sets that are large and complex, rendering traditional analysis methods inadequate. 'Large' can be defined in many ways, including both the number of discrete or atomic elements, but also, the actual size in terms of bytes can also be important [1]. A single image can be viewed as being one datum, but in other cases may be viewed to have multiple data elements (i.e. each pixel). An image can be as small as 10s of bytes, but typically is megabytes, but can be several orders of magnitude larger. Furthermore, most research requires many images, and usually further processing on each image must be done, yielding an enormous amount of data to be managed. For example, generating filtered versions of one 15 MB image can lead to several GB depending on the filters that been applied. Additionally, when the information is combined with metadata like genomic information or pathology imaging, the data increase exponentially in size [2–4].

Current popular non-medical imaging applications are as simple as determining if a certain animal is present in a picture. In some cases, medical imaging applications can be as simple: is there a cancer present in this mammogram? In most cases, though, the task is more complex: is the texture of the liver indicating hepatic steatosis, or is the abnormality seen on this brain MRI due to a high grade glioma, multiple sclerosis, a metastasis, or any of a number of other causes. In some respects, the problem is similar, but other aspects are different. The stakes are also much higher.

Medical image assessment nearly always requires other information about the patient-demographic data as well as information about family members that might help with genetically related diseases, or individual history of prior trauma or other disease. There are well-developed ontologies for describing these various entities though these are rarely used in routine clinical practice. Thus, as with other medical data mining efforts, collecting, transforming, and linking the medical record information to the images is a substantial and non-trivial effort [5].

Finally, once one has the images and appropriate medical history collected, the actual processing of the image data must begin. In many cases, multiple image types can be collected for a part of the body, and 'registering' these with each other is essential, such that a given x, y, z location in one image is the same tissue as in another image. Since most body tissues deform, this transformation is non-trivial. And tracking the tissues through time is even more challenging, particularly if the patient has had surgery or experienced other things that substantially changed their shape. Once the images are registered, one can then begin to apply more sophisticated algorithms to identify the tissues and organs within the image, and once the organs are known, one can then begin to try to determine the diagnosis.

One of the challenging tasks when dealing with big data when there are multiple associations, like medical images and metadata originating from a variety of sources, is management and curation [6]. Without proper organization, it is very challenging to extract meaningful results [7]. Big data analytics based on well-organized and linked data sets plays a significant role in aiding the exploration and discovery process as well as improving the delivery of care [8–10].

In this chapter, we describe a system we have constructed based on years of experience attempting to perform the above analysis. We believe that this system has unique properties that will serve as a basis for moving medical imaging solidly into the 'big data' world, including flexible means to represent complex data, a highly scalable storage structure for data, graphical workflows to allow users to efficiently operate on large data sets, and integration with GPU-based grid computers that are critical to computing on large image sets [11].

http://dx.doi.org/10.5772/63815

2. Unique requirements of medical image big data

2.1. Image data formats: DICOM, NIfTI, others

Most people are familiar with photographic standards for image files—JPEG, TIFF, PNG, and the like. These are designed to serve the needs of general photography, including support for RGB colour scheme, compression that saves space at the cost of perfect fidelity, and a simple header describing some of the characteristics of the photograph and camera.

Medical images share some similarity with photographic images—indeed in some cases, such as endoscopy, ophthalmology, or skin photographs use standard photographic methods. Pathology images are similar, but typically have much larger number of pixels—often billions of pixels for an image of an entire slide. Radiologic images are unique in that most are grey scale only and with a larger number of grey scales (16 bits or 65,536 grey levels) than photographic images. The result was that standards for photographic images did not support the needs of the early digital imaging modalities (which were mostly in radiology). The American College of Radiology (ACR) and the National Electrical Manufacturers Association (NEMA) recognized the increasing need for standards for exchanging digital images and developed the ACR-NEMA standard for medical images, which was released in 1985. The third version of ACR-NEMA dropped previously described hardware connection methods and focused on an information model, and exchange method that was generalized to non-radiology images and was designed to be used over standard networks. This third version was therefore renamed from 'ACR-NEMA' to 'DICOM' (Digital Communications in Medicine) [12]. The DICOM standard continues to evolve to support new imaging modalities and capabilities, and also new technical capabilities (e.g. RESTful interfaces). For many years, DICOM defined each image as its own 'object' and thus its own file. While was fine for radiographics images, it was more problematic for multi-slice image techniques like CT and MR that naturally produce images that are effectively three dimensional (3D). DICOM does support 3D image formats and also image annotation methods, but adoption of these has been slow, leading to use of other file formats for imaging research [13].

An early popular file format for medical image research was the Analyze© file format which had one small (384 bytes) header file, and a separate file which consisted of only image pixel data. The header proved too limiting for some uses, specifically its representation of image orientation, and was extended, resulting in the Neuroimaging Informatics Technology Initiative (NIfTI) file format (see http://brainder.org/2012/09/23/the-nifti-file-format/). There are other formats including Nearly Raw Raster Data (NRRD) (see http://teem.sourceforge.net/nrrd/index.html) that are also used in medical image research.

In most cases, each file format is able to represent the relevant information fairly well. There are many tools to convert between the various formats. The main advantage of these alternative formats is that a complete three or more dimensional data set is stored in a single file, compared to the popular 2D DICOM option which can requires many 10s to 1000s of files. Which file is selected is largely driven by the applications one expects to use, and the file formats they support.

2.2. Connecting images with image-specific metadata and other data

One of the major concerns when managing big data originating from medical practice is the data privacy. Data privacy is a critical issue for all people, but in most jurisdictions, there are specific requirements for how medical and health information must be kept private. One of the early comprehensive regulations on medical data privacy was the Health Insurance Portability and Accountability Act (HIPAA) [14]. It specified what data were considered private and could not be exposed without patient consent, and penalties for when such data breeches occurred. In the case of textual medical data, even a casual reader can quickly determine if protected Health Information (PHI) is within a document.

Medical images are more difficult to assess because DICOM images contain tags as part of the header that are populated with PHI during the normal course of an imaging examination. Releasing such medical images with that information in tact without patient consent would represent a breech of HIPAA. Removing these tags, and inserting some other identifier such as for research is straightforward to do in most cases. However, in some cases, vendors may also place PHI in non-standard locations of the header or may include it as part of the pixel information in the image. In some cases, this is done for compatibility with older software. In other cases, hospitals have been known to put PHI in fields that were designated for other purposes, to address their unique workflow needs. It is these exceptional cases that make de-identification more challenging. Fortunately, putting PHI into non-standard locations is declining as awareness of these problems is becoming better known.

Medical images may also contain PHI that is ‘burned into’ pixels—that is, the displayed image shows the PHI. While easily recognized by humans, it is more difficult for computers to recognize such PHI. One may use Optical Character Recognition algorithms, but they may have false negatives and positives due to the actual image contents looking like a character, or obscuring a character. Fortunately, the practice of burning in PHI is also declining.

When study of big data is conducted for clinical purposes, it may be appropriate to perform the research directly on medical records with the true medical record identifiers. This avoids the need for de-identification, which can be slow and expensive for some types of data. The medical record number usually makes it easy to tie various pieces of information for a subject together. However, having PHI directly accessible by computer systems beyond the Electronic Health Record (EHR) [15,16] represents increased risk of HIPAA or equivalent violation and therefore is discouraged.

Working on de-identified data substantially reduces the risk of releasing PHI during the course of big data research. This means that the de-identification step must be tailored for the type of data and that the de-identification also be coordinated so that the same study identifier is used. While not complex in concept, implementation can be more difficult if there is a strong need for rapid data access. The challenge is that when a new patient arrives in an emergency room, their true identity may not be known for some time, but medical tests and notes will be generated with a ‘temporary ID’. How and when that temporary ID is changed to the final ID can be very different, and in some cases, a single temporary ID cannot be used in all systems.

http://dx.doi.org/10.5772/63815

Misidentified patients (e.g. same name) and correction of their data are similar problems. And cases where there is more than one subject (e.g. the foetus in a mother) also represent challenges that are manageable but must be considered up front. Obstetrical ultrasound images are nearly always of the foetus, but usually are collected under the identifier of the mother. In the case of twins, it can be challenging to know which foetus is seen on a given image, and such a notation is usually done by annotating the image (burning into pixels) rather than in a defined tag that is reliably computed.

2.3. Computational environment

Currently, there is no standard or expected computational environment used for image and metadata analysis. Researchers utilize a variety of operating systems, programming languages, and libraries (and versions of libraries). Furthermore, the tools can be deployed as command line executable, GUIs or more recently as web-based applications. There is a plethora of computational tools available but setting them up and maintaining them poses challenges. Setting up the appropriate environment is challenging since the user has to anticipate all the specific libraries and parameters that will be used during later computational steps. This is made more challenging because not all tools are available on any single platform. There is also an expectation of sharing data and algorithms, which also complicates long-term support of a platform.

Computation on medical images is very different from computation on other data types [17]. The fundamental unit in a medical image is the pixel, and the operations are those used in image processing elsewhere: filtering, artefact correction, registration/alignment, and segmentation to name a few [18]. Medical image analysis techniques are aimed in quantification of disease, image enhancement, detection of changes, or more generally dealing with medical image based problems originating from different imaging modalities utilizing digital image analysis techniques [18,19]. While these computations are unique to imaging, later steps that include classification and characterization or more generally analytical methods are similar to other big data efforts originating from different fields [20].

3. PESSCARA design

We have developed the Platform to Enable Sharing of Scientific Computing Algorithms and Research Assets (PESSCARA) to address the challenges we see with big data in medical imaging. The central component of PESSCARA is a Content Management System (CMS) that stores image data and metadata as objects. The CMS we chose is TACTIC (http://www.southpawtech.com), an open-source CMS with a Python API to access objects [21]. The Python API allows efficient development and testing of image processing routines on large sets of image objects [22]. TACTIC manages both project data and files, with project data stored in the database and files stored in the file system. TACTIC can store any type of data and image data format, including file formats commonly used in medical research, such as Analyze, NRRD, NifTI, and DICOM. The properties assigned to the image objects can be used to select the subset of images to be processed, define the way that images are processed, and to capture some or all of the results of processing. TACTIC also has a workflow engine that can execute a series of graphically defined steps. Finally, it has project management facilities that can address planning, data auditing, and other aspects of project management.

To assist communication with the computational environment, we developed a Python library (tiPY) that facilitates input and output from TACTIC (**Figure 1**). PESSCARA is the first system that provides the research community with an environment suitable to deal with the requirements of medical image analysis while supporting the spirit of open and accountable research.

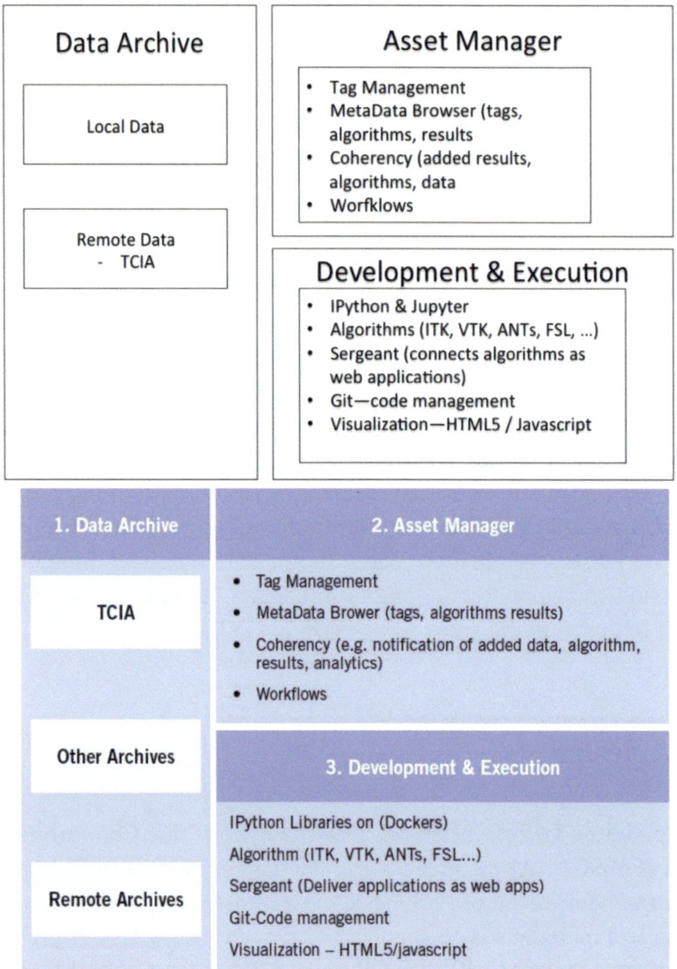

Figure 1. PESSCARA architecture. Most image analysis systems consist only of a data archive. PESSCARA includes this and allows for both federated and local data archives. PESSCARA also has an Asset Manager that allows flexible tagging of data, easy browsing of the data, and a workflow engine for processing data based on tags. Workflows and components of workflows are created in the development environment, and workflows are also executed in that same environment.

http://dx.doi.org/10.5772/63815

3.1. Databases vs content management

Databases are widely used for storing data. Although the main technology behind a CMS is essentially a database, in a CMS the content is not just a retrievable object, but also is an asset with properties. Such an object can be examined and displayed based on its properties, and based on those properties, it can be related to any other asset in the CMS. These additional capabilities make a CMS an excellent tool to use for big data research, since such data are complex and require metadata in order to assure proper processing and interpretation, thus leading to meaningful information [6,23].

PESSCARA is designed to link image and associated metadata with the computational environment. It allows users to focus on the content rather than database tables and gives great flexibility in assigning meaning to the various assets. Content in our example (discussed later in this chapter) consists of image data, metadata, biomarker information, notes, and tags.

TACTIC tracks the content creation process, which in the case of medical image research means the original acquired image, and all of its subsequent processing steps until the final measured version. TACTIC allows tracking of data check-in and checkout by providing a mechanism to identify changes; it also employs a versioning system to record the history of the changes to specific content. It also includes user logins and authentication, allowing tracking of who performed certain steps and when. Our adaptation of TACTIC for medical image research purposes was straightforward because medical images are digital content.

PESSCARA has a very flexible data-handling schema (**Figure 2**) that can easily address the heterogeneous data that are a part of 'big data', so it can adapt as new requirements emerge. It is easy to add other components to this schema to address other needs, for instance when genomic data need to be processed, rather than simply included as data.

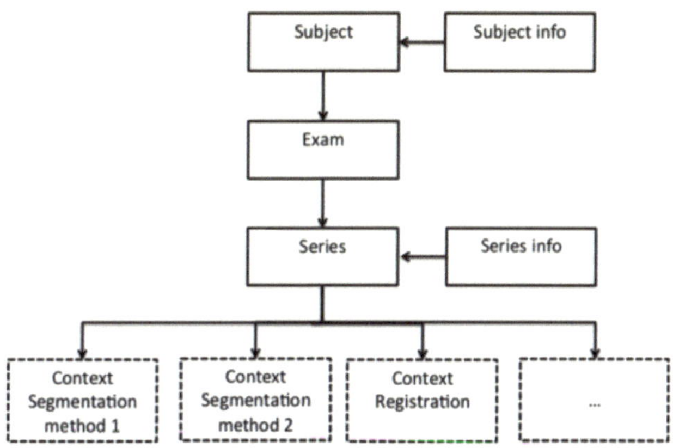

Figure 2. Data-handling schema. PESSCARA allows tags to be created for any object of group of objects. We established the basic organization of PESSCARA to have consistent tags at the Subject, Exam, Series, and Image level. There is also a 'study' level tag that equates to the institutional research board identifier, or essentially the project number. Each of these has a context that has permitted methods and workflows that can be applied.

All the data are available through a Representational State (REST) API designed to scale based on the requests issued from the analytical applications. Some of this is a part of TACTIC, though more of the management of computational tasks is through other components like sergeant and the grid engine (see **Figure 1**).

3.2. Workflow

When dealing with a large number of assets (data and metadata of any kind), it is crucial to have a mechanism that can automate and efficiently execute a specific series of actions on the data. In general, the workflows in medical imaging research tend to be linear and simple to implement. For example, a data importation/curation task typically begins by classifying the incoming image data based on their type, converting the data to a format suitable for subsequent analyses, placing new images on a queue for human quality control where the system then displays selected images and enables the reviewer to approve or reject them.

PESSCARA supports such workflows, which may be developed either as Python code, or developed graphically using the provided tool (**Figure 3**). PESSCARA users may design workflows and set the events that trigger workflows and define the users who are allowed to perform human steps. Tasks within the workflow can be calls to REST APIs, Python code, or notifications.

The workflows can be initialized based on events that can be either automated or manually controlled by a user or a prespecified group.

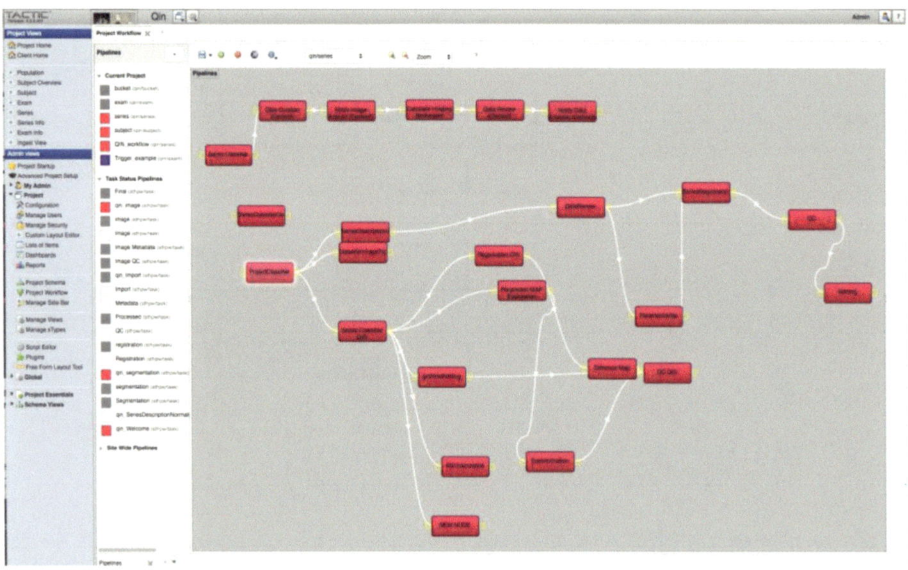

Figure 3. Snapshot of the pipeline creation tool. The pipeline workflow is used to depict the steps that a particular series need to undergo.

http://dx.doi.org/10.5772/63815

3.3. Grid computing

PESSCARA currently leverages the power of grid computing utilizing *sergeant* (https://github.com/potis/sergeant), which is an open-source tool that enables the deployment of code as web apps. This enables easy scalability, since the web app can be hosted on a cloud-based infrastructure design. Sergeant offers the ability to interact with each web app through a REST API, making it easier for people to utilize an application without the hustle of setting up and configuring binaries or executable. In the case of PESSCARA, a 'step' can be a call to sergeant, which in turn, could launch a grid job that might result in the processing of a large group of images utilizing the grid engine. This is, in fact, a common thing for us to do in our research efforts.

Cloud computing has been emerging as a good way to address computational challenges in modern big data research. This is because it is a way that a small research laboratory can access large computers, and the pay-as-you-go model provides flexibility for any size user. Cloud computing also addresses one of the challenges relating to transferring and sharing data, because data sets and analysis results held in the cloud can be shared with others just by providing credentials so they may also access the instance in the cloud.

The PESSCARA design allows us to leverage such cloud-computing resources. PESSCARA is engineered to support architectures such as MapReduce, Spark, and Storm [24–26] that are popular constructs in cloud computing. These technologies enable researchers to utilize data for fast analysis, with the end goal to translate scientific discovery into applications for clinical settings.

3.4. Multi-site synchronization

Content synchronization is an important requirement for multi-centre clinical trials and settings with multiple collaborators. TACTIC offers a powerful mechanism to synchronize data among servers hosting the databases and users, ensuring that changes are always up to date and that the correct version of the content is used. Encryption and decryption through a public- and private-key mechanism are used for all data transfers.

This is a particularly important feature for scientists, since 'data' include not just the raw data, but also all the metadata (which can be at least as laborious to create) and processed versions of data. PESSCARA achieves this via the content management system using the object capabilities, meaning that the visibility of what is shared and synchronized is very flexible and straightforward to administer.

We decided NOT to use this synchronization for algorithms, primarily because other tools such as github (www.github.com) already provide this capability, and specialized capabilities like merging of code—something that is not as easily done with a CMS, unless a special module was written for 'code' objects. Since github has already done this, we preferred to let users select the tool of their choice for code sharing and management.

4. Using PESSCARA

4.1. Data importation, curation, editing

PESSCARA incorporates dcm4che (http://www.dcm4che.org/) for DICOM connectivity and the Clinical Trial Processor (CTP) (https://www.rsna.org/ctp.aspx) for DICOM de-identification. The dcm4che module is an open-source Java library used as the DICOM receiver. The receiver can receive the images from a picture archiving and communications system or directly from the particular imaging modality.

Subsequently, CTP is used to de-identify the data for compliance with HIPAA. Tags that should be removed from the DICOM object are configured through a lookup table. In addition, CTP provides a log of all actions, which meets the logging requirements in 21 CFR part 11. During the de-identification process, a table with the correspondence between patient identifier and research identifier is kept and securely maintained. This table is useful for adding information to the patient dataset, such as tags from the pathology reports and survival information. In addition, when data corresponding to follow-up studies of patients who have been de-identified are included, CTP will assign the same research identifiers. Although CTP is capable of removing PHI, it can appear in many unexpected locations (e.g. burned-in pixel values). For this reason, PESSCARA is typically configured to place imported images in a 'quarantine' zone until the assigned user reviews the data. In our case, an important step of image importation is converting images from DICOM to NIfTI because most image processing packages do not deal well with native DICOM files. The tiPY library includes a routine to perform this conversion.

Once data have been imported into TACTIC and some initial workflows have been completed (i.e. for image series classification, or querying databases to gather additional information such as genomics or survival information), TACTIC workflow places the object on a queue for data quality inspection. At this point, information missing can be added manually, and poor quality items can be censored.

The project management element of PESCARA enables project managers to monitor resource usage and progress. This can allow tracking of resources used to support accurate billing and know individual effort. One can also assign total expected counts and thus calculate fractional completion.

To ensure data security, PESSCARA regularly backs up all parameter files used by CTP, dcm4che, the virtual machine running TACTIC, and the file storage area. This exists as just another workflow and thus is flexible in what is included, frequency, and how it is performed.

4.2. Creating image processing modules/dockers

Distribution of image analysis algorithms, particularly when developed in small research laboratories, is challenging since currently there is not standardized image analysis development environment. When the user employs the PESSCARA infrastructure, they are working with a standardized environment that usually enables easy deployment of the algorithm.

http://dx.doi.org/10.5772/63815

However, for algorithms that are not easy to be implemented in the PESSCARA environment (i.e. the LINUX host running PESSCARA), there is support for docker containers (http://www.docker.com) to perform 'steps' of a workflow.

Just as sergeant is able to 'request' execution of steps through a REST API that might result in submission of jobs to a grid engine, it is possible to 'request' the instantiation of a docker container that could perform a given step. The benefit of a docker container is that the execution environment is defined by the docker creator and is allowed to be different from the host environment. Virtual machines also have this benefit, but virtual machines require much more computer resource to execute. A disadvantage is that currently Microsoft Windows and Apple OS X applications are not supported; though, Windows support has been announced.

For development purposes, PESSCARA supports a majority of tools used in the image processing community, including ITK, Slicer3D, FSL, and others. However, for algorithm development, Python is the preferred language for PESSCARA. Python is a very approachable, readable language that includes a number of powerful tools including Numpy, Matplotlib, scikit-learn, nipype, RPy, and pandas. The Jupyter Notebook development framework extends Python and is at the core of a substantial shift in the methodology of science, enabling iteration, documentation, and sharing of science. This philosophy is in perfect alignment with PESSCARA. It promotes reproducible research (i.e. provenance tracking of the entire history from input data, algorithms used, intermediate calculations, and results). Its interactive capabilities means that code that code already run can have its results used rather than re-running the code.

While Python is the 'first language' of PESSCARA, there are many libraries and developers that depend on other languages, including non-Python tools such as ITK, FSL, ANTs, Slicer, and others. Furthermore, Jupyter enables development in many different languages including R, C++, and Julia. [27].

A Jupyter Notebook (which includes code, data, and results) can be easily shared by simply giving the URL and login credentials to your audience. In addition, the Results/Output and comments (including LaTex and Markdown) can be integrated into the Notebook to document what has been done in a long-term and shareable way.

The basic model for such 'shared science' is import/export. The user often starts by importing other investigators' Notebooks, but they may also start their own. They can then develop in their own 'sandbox', and when they feel they have something to share, they can 'export' it, which makes it publicly visible and available to be imported by others. Exporting the code in conventional Python format is also supported. They can also save all code and results as HTML for publishing on the web, or as PDF as a 'final' document to be saved in an electronic laboratory notebook [28].

Based on this architecture, the algorithms can be utilized by a variety of cloud services and important characteristic to consider when large amount of data are involved.

4.3. Creating and executing workflows

As noted above, workflow is critical in modern science. One must be able to execute the research process consistently. When dealing with 'big data', efficiency is also essential. In the following section, we show a multi-centre implementation of a workflow created with PESSCARA (**Figure 4**). The application will be aimed at developing imaging biomarkers for differentiating between progression and pseudoprogressions in case of glioblastoma multiforme (a type of malignant brain tumour) using large data sets and then applying the findings from a large data set to a live clinical trial and ultimately routine clinical practice.

We see PESSCARA having two configurations: one for development and one for clinical trials or practice. The development configuration includes the CMS system with the data used for development as well as a large batch-oriented computational environment. Once the code and the workflows have been established, the clinical configuration is created containing only the workflows and the computational environed to support them.

Following is an example of how the two configurations of PESSCARA can work.

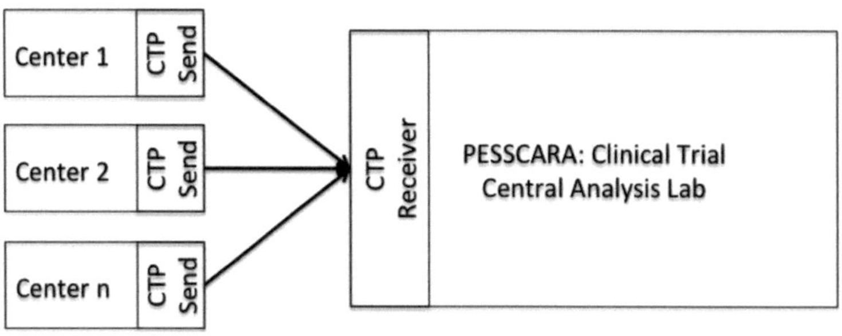

Figure 4. Translation of workflows created with PESSCARA for a multi-centre set-up. Each of n Centers collects image data and sends via CTP software. The same CTP software also acts as a receiver at the Central Analysis Lab, where CTP sends it to PESSCARA for analysis. We expect there would be a separate instance of PESSCARA for a clinical trial to minimize the chance that a developer would alter data or impact performance.

Researchers from the participating institutions can use the PESSCARA development configuration to develop the image analysis algorithms as well as the workflows necessary to compute the image-based biomarker. Typically, data from multiple centres are used for analysis. Both development and clinical trial configurations will typically have an input process where data are reviewed for quality and then stored. In the case shown in **Figure 5**, we imagine that Center 3 is responsible for curating the data, and after that, Center 2 will perform visual QC of image quality and automated image segmentation. Center 3 then reviews Center 2's work, and Center 1 is notified that data analysis is complete. In the development configuration, there is a loop where Center 1 along with other centres may refine the analysis, and further computational models/biomarkers are tested. When the workflow is completed and the supporting web app established the PESSCARA, clinical trial configuration is created.

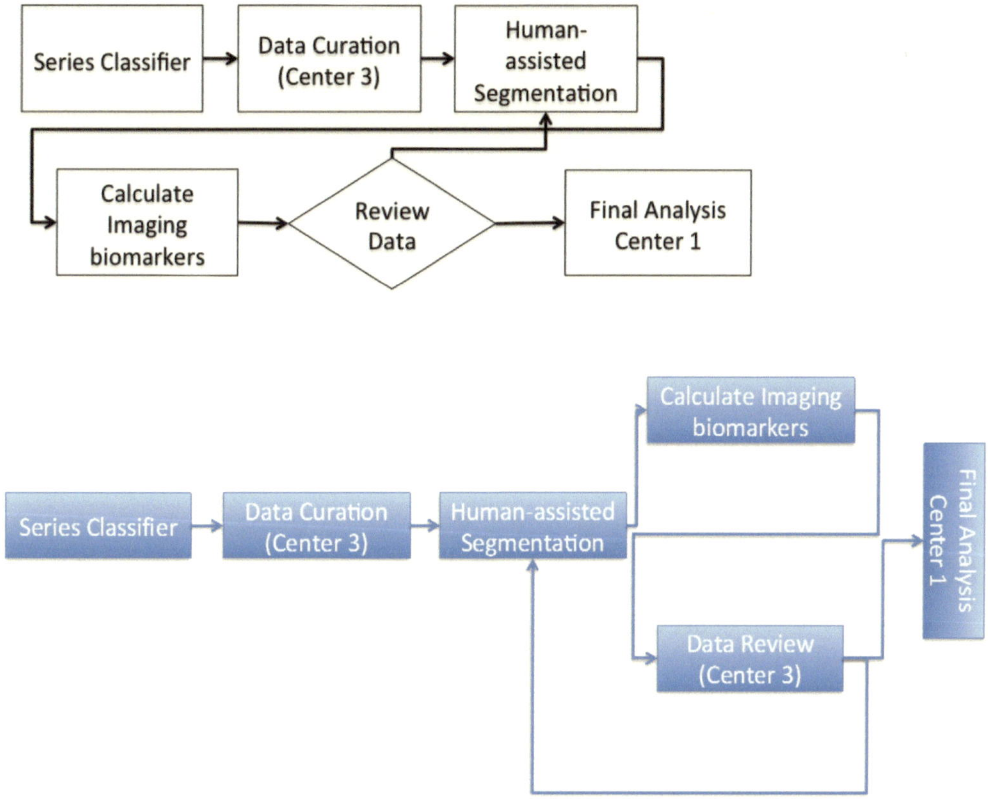

Figure 5. Example workflow. In this case, images are first identified by the Series Classifier. Once they are labelled, Data Curation is performed, in this example at a remote centre (Center 3). Then, human-assisted segmentation is performed, and biomarkers and then computed. This is again reviewed by a human, and if acceptable, the measurements are sent to the central data collection.

The clinical trial configuration is focused on efficient calculation of a biomarker developed via the above mechanism, and in some cases, it also provides a mechanism for immediate delivery of the biomarker result. As with development, when a subject has been identified in Center 1 as suitable for the study, it is forwarded to the PESSCARA DICOM receiver set-up for this study. The dataset PHI are de-identified through use of the CTP functionality and a preconfigured CTP configuration file. All the received files are placed in a folder, where they are 'ingested'. The metadata are also forwarded to the system utilizing the tiPY library. A configuration file exists in the receiving pool to assign the proper tags to the data to be ingested, such as institutional review board number, data type, and project name. The ingesting process will create a new entry inside TACTIC or will update the information if the data already exist. Once the data have been injected, a Series workflow is triggered. The first step of the workflow is a classifier step, which routes the data for a specific study to the right pipeline—for instance, that an image series designed to measure perfusion is sent to an algorithm that calculates perfusion. Subsequently, DICOM field tags are extracted and a normalized series description is assigned to each object (e.g. 'Axial', 'T1', and 'Post-Contrast' might all be assigned to an axial postcontrast T1 image). If the classifier finds all the required series (T1 weighted postcontrast and perfusion in this case), a notification is send to the centre responsible for data curation). Otherwise, a notification/report of the data missing is send to the predesigned contact person in the originating centre.

Once data curation is finished, a notification is sent to centre 2 where the tumour segmentation is performed. The Image analyst can get the data either through the web page or through a link, to perform the tumour segmentation task. Once this is completed, the step(s) responsible for perfusion analysis computation as well as the registration of the tumour ROI to the perfusion image is executed. Once the data are reviewed and found acceptable, the imaging biomarkers extracted from perfusion are assigned to the appropriate tags for that examination. Once this step in completed, the data metadata and all analytics extracted are available for analysis utilizing any kind of 'big data' analysis methodology. This may be simply stored for later group analysis or may be made available for immediate clinical decision-making. All the data and metadata created during the execution of the workflow are backed up to a different server for protection over data loss.

4.4. Current status and next steps

Currently, the system is under development with further optimization needed to enhance its security features. Additionally, further resources are needed to provide the users with more resources for faster testing and support for algorithms with higher computational requirements. The system has been undergoing rapid development—the documentation and training resources have not kept up.

We hope that the next phases will see further connections of PESSCARA with non-imaging data repositories; improvements in the workflow engine enable a wider variety of algorithms on a wider variety of platforms and greater connections to clinical systems.

We do intend to provide the basic system as open access tools through github so researchers will be able to set the same environment locally with more resources. We also hope to provide a simple demonstration environment (http://www.PESSCARA.org) that will allow prospective users to test the PESSCARA environment.

5. Conclusion

Big data techniques will lead to an improved model of healthcare delivery with the potential to achieve better clinical outcomes and increased efficiency. However, appropriate infrastructure is needed to enable the data collection and curation especially in case of heterogeneous (with respect to data) environments such as healthcare.

PESSCARA aims to minimize the requirements for data downloading and transfer, since data and metadata are hosted within the same infrastructure. Code development also can be performed through a web interface making the system easy to use for inexperienced users. Perhaps even more important is that researchers can share their algorithms—the analysis

http://dx.doi.org/10.5772/63815

performed, and the subsequent results—which is a significant step toward reproducible research. When big data originate from multimodal data that have complex connections to other data, the use of a CMS is a must. PESSCARA is and will continue to meet the unique demands of big data research in medical imaging by leveraging a good CMS that is effectively connected to powerful computational resources, and an algorithm development environment designed for code and result sharing. 'Shared Science' is the future of science, and PESSCARA is one tool for medical imaging to participate in this new world of big data and shared science.

Acknowledgements

This work was supported by NIH Grant CA160045.

Author details

Panagiotis Korfiatis and Bradley Erickson*

*Address all correspondence to: bje@mayo.edu

Department of Radiology, Mayo Clinic, Rochester, MN, United States

References

[1] Jagadish HV. Big data and science: myths and reality. Big Data Res. 2015 June;2(2):49–52.

[2] Tan SS, Gao G, Koch S. Big data and analytics in healthcare. Methods Inf Med. 2015 November 27;54(6):546–7. PubMed PMID: 26577624.

[3] Belle A, Thiagarajan R, Soroushmehr SM, Navidi F, Beard DA, Najarian K. Big data analytics in healthcare. Biomed Res Int. 2015;2015:370194. PubMed PMID: 26229957. PMCID: PMC4503556.

[4] Langer SG. Challenges for data storage in medical imaging research. J Digit Imaging. 2011 April;24(2):203–7. PubMed PMID: 20544372. PMCID: PMC3056978.

[5] Prather JC, Lobach DF, Goodwin LK, Hales JW, Hage ML, Hammond WE. Medical data mining: knowledge discovery in a clinical data warehouse. Proceedings of AMIA Annual Fall Symposium. 1997:101–5. PubMed PMID: 9357597. PMCID: PMC2233405.

[6] Lynch C. Big data: how do your data grow? Nature. 2008 September 4;455(7209):28–9. PubMed PMID: WOS:000258890200019 [English].

[7] Mathew P, Pillai A. Big data challenges and solutions in healthcare: a survey. In: Snášel V, Abraham A, Krömer P, Pant M, Muda AK, editors. Innovations in Bio-Inspired Computing and Applications. Advances in Intelligent Systems and Computing. 424: Springer International Publishing; 2016. p. 543–53.

[8] Raghupathi W, Raghupathi V. Big data analytics in healthcare: promise and potential. Health Inf Sci Syst. 2014;2:3. PubMed PMID: 25825667. PMCID: PMC4341817.

[9] Trifonova OP, Il'in VA, Kolker EV, Lisitsa AV. Big data in biology and medicine: based on material from a joint workshop with representatives of the international Data-Enabled Life Science Alliance, July 4, 2013, Moscow, Russia. Acta Nat. 2013 July;5(3): 13–6. PubMed PMID: 24303199. PMCID: PMC3848064.

[10] Margolis R, Derr L, Dunn M, Huerta M, Larkin J, Sheehan J, et al. The National Institutes of Health's Big Data to Knowledge (BD2K) initiative: capitalizing on biomedical big data. J Am Med Inform Assoc. 2014 November–December;21(6):957–8. PubMed PMID: 25008006. PMCID: PMC4215061.

[11] Schadt EE, Linderman MD, Sorenson J, Lee L, Nolan GP. Computational solutions to large-scale data management and analysis. Nat Rev Genet. 2010 September;11(9):647–57. PubMed PMID: 20717155. PMCID: PMC3124937.

[12] National Electrical Manufacturers Association, American College of Radiology. Digital imaging and communications in medicine (DICOM). Washington, DC: National Electrical Manufacturers Association; 1998. vol. 1–8, p. 10–5.

[13] Larobina M, Murino L. Medical image file formats. J Digit Imaging. 2014 April;27(2): 200–6. PubMed PMID: 24338090. PMCID: PMC3948928.

[14] Services USDoHH. U.S. Department of Health & Human Services [cited 2016 01/01/2016]. Available from: http://www.hhs.gov/ocr/privacy/hipaa/understanding/summary/.

[15] Hamilton B. Electronic Health Records. 3rd ed. New York: McGraw-Hill; 2013.

[16] Carter JH, American College of Physicians. Electronic Health Records: A Guide for Clinicians and Administrators. 2nd ed. Philadelphia: ACP Press; 2008. vol. xxi, 530 p.

[17] Duncan JS, Ayache N. Medical image analysis: Progress over two decades and the challenges ahead. IEEE Trans Pattern Anal. 2000 January;22(1):85–106. PubMed PMID: WOS:000085472300005 [English].

[18] Dhawan AP. Medical Image Analysis. Hoboken, NJ, Piscataway, NJ: Wiley-Interscience, IEEE Press; 2003. vol. xv, 315p.

[19] Costaridou L. Medical Image Analysis Methods. Boca Raton: CRC Press/Taylor & Francis; 2005. 489p.

[20] Mohammed EA, Far BH, Naugler C. Applications of the MapReduce programming framework to clinical big data analysis: current landscape and future trends. BioData Min. 2014;7:22. PubMed PMID: 25383096. PMCID: PMC4224309.

[21] Technology S. TACTIC Digital Asset and Workflow Software [cited 2014 01/01/2016].

[22] Korfiatis PD, Kline TL, Blezek DJ, Langer SG, Ryan WJ, Erickson BJ. MIRMAID: a content management system for medical image analysis research. Radiographics. 2015 September–October;35(5):1461–8. PubMed PMID: 26284301. PMCID: PMC4613872.

[23] Chen JC, Chen YG, Du XY, Li CP, Lu JH, Zhao SY, et al. Big data challenge: a data management perspective. Front Comput Sci-Chi. 2013 April;7(2):157–64. PubMed PMID: WOS:000317303800001 [English].

[24] Richter AN, Khoshgoftaar TM, Landset S, Hasanin T, editors. A multi-dimensional comparison of toolkits for machine learning with big data. In: 2015 IEEE International Conference on Information Reuse and Integration (IRI), 13–15 August, 2015.

[25] Sun Z, Chen F, Chi M, Zhu Y. A spark-based big data platform for massive remote sensing data processing. In: Zhang C, Huang W, Shi Y, Yu PS, Zhu Y, Tian Y, et al., editors. Data Science. Lecture Notes in Computer Science. 9208: Springer International Publishing; 2015. p. 120–6.

[26] Dean J, Ghemawat S. Mapreduce: simplified data processing on large clusters. Commun ACM. 2008 January;51(1):107–13. PubMed PMID: WOS:000251994700031 [English].

[27] Perez F, Granger BE. IPython: A system for interactive scientific computing. Comput Sci Eng. 2007 May–June;9(3):21–9. PubMed PMID: WOS:000245668100005 [English].

[28] Shen H. Interactive notebooks: sharing the code. Nature. 2014 November 6;515(7525): 151–2. PubMed PMID: 25373681.